DISSOCIATIVE IDENTITY DISORDER

Basics from a Christian Perspective

Dr. Lynda L. Irons

This book is dedicated to those who wrestle with dissociation in themselves or in someone they love. I am grateful for the holy privilege of having worked with hundreds of precious, courageous, funny, and deeply spiritual dissociative people over the past twenty-five years. Thank you for taking the risk in your pursuit of healing by becoming transparent and vulnerable during ministry sessions.

Dr. Lynda L. Irons

TABLE OF CONTENTS PAGE

Dr. Lynda L. Irons

INTRODUCTION

Dissociative Identity Disorder was formerly known as Multiple Personality Disorder. Many counselors dislike the term "disorder" and agree with the experts who assert that dissociation is a coping skill that was used of necessity to attempt to bring some order to the disordered circumstances and dysfunctional relationships.

Disorder should more rightfully describe the chaotic family of origin or the perverse perpetrator or the traumatic situation and not the victim of such things. To label the child who experienced these incomprehensible events or lifestyles is to discredit their creative, ingenious way of making sense out of a senseless world.

Dissociation is an accurate description of both brain function and the functions of the mind. Dissociation resolves, at least temporarily, the intolerable conflicts that a child cannot be expected to sort out given her insufficient power, limited intellect, inadequate resources, and scant options.

This book has been written in response to the hundreds of requests for basic information about dissociation. May those who are dissociative or know someone who is dissociative on some level be able to recognize themselves or others they love on these pages and be encouraged that they are not crazy; they are not mentally ill; they are not hopeless or helpless.

It is not my goal to diagnose, nor do I possess the credentials to diagnose; but it is my goal to make sound conclusions based on accurate observations. It is my desire that those who are dissociative will do the same and find hope and direction for resolving the issues that made dissociation necessary in the first place.

1

OVERVIEW

$\mathfrak{D}$addy removed his belt as he quickly moved towards Jane. His countenance was fierce as he barked out the words, "Get over here!" Even if Jane had wanted to obey, she had no strength left in her body. She had nothing left in her heart after years of abuse. Her lack of obedience further inflamed daddy's fury. While he lashed at her inert body, Jane's eyes stared at the cup she had dropped. Inside, however, she was staring at something beyond that. She floated into her sweet, safe place. It was a place her daddy could never touch.

Mary loved playing with her little granddaughter at the park. One day she realized as she was in the tube that she was the only grandmother going down the slide. Then she heard a voice inside her head like that of a four-year-old, "My body seems too big for this."

A young woman confessed, "Sometimes I feel like a by-stander watching myself. Other times I feel like I was in a dream, asleep. Was I asleep while I was there?"

An eight-year-old got into an argument with her friend. It attracted the attention of everyone in the church basement. They witnessed her angrily shove her friend down three steps and then immediately rush down after her saying, "Are you, all right?" She was shocked and upset when the fallen friend said, "You pushed me! Get away!" The confused little girl continued to deny her actions. Her mother later remarked that she was either the best liar in the world or the best actress after the child's continued denials.

A young man terrified of circumstances surrounding him imagined a thick metal door that he pulled shut. It trapped any other memory or thought on the other side. He retreated behind that door when he felt intimidated by life. He had many gaps in his memory that ranged from minutes or hours to an entire year of grade school.

A teenager admitted, "I daydream a lot."

One man admitted, "I feel like Dr. Jekyll and Mr. Hyde."

Another man asserted, "I hate my job, but I do it very well." Minutes later he said, "I've been put on administrative leave for a week."

A woman noted, "Lots of times when I'm driving, I'm alarmed because I just went through an intersection and I don't know if it was a red light or a green light."

These are just a few examples of people who made statements and observations about themselves. They describe an experience which falls somewhere on the continuum of dissociation. Some are on the "normal" end of the continuum while others move down the line toward more significant dissociation.

We interact with people like this every day. We are related to them; we work with them. They are not freaks; they are not mentally ill. They have displayed the use of a marvelous coping skill to one degree or another.

Most of them will never know that they are displaying some level of dissociation that is a bit beyond the norm. They would never need to seek professional help to resolve it. It may be discovered while dealing with other issues. Others are aware that they have a problem, but they just do not know what it is.

Dissociative Identity Disorder was formerly known as Multiple Personality Disorder. It was considered to be very rare. People who were labeled with MPD were treated as freaks and someone to be afraid of or else they were institutionalized in a mental health unit.

Many mental health care workers were unfamiliar with or unable to detect its presence in these people because of the mysterious symptoms. Those patients were often labeled with an array of alarming psychiatric diagnoses such as schizophrenia, bipolar disorder, and various personality disorders based on whatever behavior was observed. The diagnosis would then generate corresponding pharmaceuticals.

In 1994, the psychiatric community renamed it Dissociative Identity Disorder. That has been somewhat helpful in removing the stigma from the diagnosis. It was, and is, still considered to be rare in the mental health community, but that is changing. Until recently, the mental health workers in some states were not permitted to use that designation; therefore, many people were misdiagnosed and given medications for that misdiagnosis.

Dissociation itself is not treatable with medication. However, people who are dissociated commonly suffer from an array of other conditions such as depression, sexual issues, panic or anxiety, eating disorders, addictions, and more. These will compound and confound anyone who is attempting to treat them or to minister to them. Those diagnoses will likely be treated with medication which may mute or mask the dissociation.

How tragic that, even when properly diagnosed, these people were getting very little effective treatment. Many experts in the mental health community said that it would take years of therapy to get someone to the point of just being functional. They offered little or no hope for complete healing and wholeness.

For a long time, there was little recognition that there are varying degrees of dissociation as well as different types of dissociation. One may be dissociative without having Dissociative Identity Disorder. *This cannot be stressed enough.* The dissociation continuum will be discussed in more detail later in this study and will help clarify different degrees and different types of dissociation that may be presented.

Most of the people with DID are females. This may be largely because of the structure of the human brain. It contains two hemispheres. When males are in the womb, there is a testosterone wash that severs many of the connections between the two hemispheres. That makes it neurologically more difficult for males to dissociate, however, many still dissociate if they have enough dissociative ability, are young enough, and traumatized deeply enough.

For the sake of brevity, I will be somewhat politically incorrect in this work by referring to those with DID as "she" or "her"' and use the generic name "Jane" in the examples and prayers. Please understand that the principles will apply to males as well.

The following questions are some of the most common which are asked about dissociative identity disorder. A brief answer will be given here. These and other questions will be answered more fully in the study.

What causes dissociation?

Most commonly, it is early chronic or acute trauma, generally prior to age six or seven, and usually of a sexual nature.

How do I know that I am dealing with DID?

The most classic signs are reports of loss of time and hearing internal conversations, that is, voices that come from inside of her head.

How do I broach the subject with the person?

Allow the Holy Spirit to guide you. It's different with each person. Sometimes she will give you hints and pray that you will notice, sometimes she does not know that she dissociates and when you educate her, she sees that she fits the profile.

How do I deal with the different personalities?

Pray. Negotiate. Respect. Believe. Love. Deal with each alternative personality (alter) as you would deal with any other individual.

Which personality is the real one?

They are all real. All of the personalities together comprise the original person prior to the trauma(s) that made dissociation necessary.

Is dissociation reversible?

Yes. When the cause for the dissociation is resolved, dissociative barriers will no longer be needed and the personalities can integrate.

What does integration look like? How does it happen?

God is gracious to customize integration for each person. It is less traumatic for the person if the dissociated parts which are to be integrated are healed first. Sometimes it is spontaneous; sometimes it is intentional.

Is DID real?

Yes. In fact, as previously stated, everyone dissociates on some level. One can be dissociative without being DID. (You are dissociating right now on a normal level.)

Is it demonic?

Absolutely not. The alternate personalities (alters) are not demons. Demons may mimic alters or the original person. Demons may oppress them, but they are no different than non-DID believers who are demonized as a result of sin by or against them, or as a result of some level of trauma (which is the result of sin).

There are many professionals who have the training and credentials to diagnose mental illnesses and/or psychiatric conditions. Most of us do not. However, we are all able to make objective observations. Those observations may lead us to conclude that a person we know has traits and characteristics that are consistent with some level of dissociation. Once the dissociation is discovered and understood, it becomes less of a mystery and thus effective treatment of and/or ministry to the dissociative person becomes possible.

2

SURVIVING BY DISSOCIATION

Dissociation on any level is a God-given coping mechanism. It allows us to think, create, pray, and much more while doing mundane, habitual chores. How tedious it would be if we had to focus on each facet of each task! Typing a document would be ultra-slow if you had to think of each key-stroke as you pressed it.

Think of all the mundane tasks (vacuuming the house, driving, jogging, etc.) that must be done daily. What a gift to be able to engage in other meaningful mental activities at the same time! Your ability to read this while being aware of an itch on your toe, an aroma wafting out of the kitchen, and various background sights and sounds is an example of normal dissociation.

"Highway hypnosis" is another common example. You drive automatically while focused on thoughts or conversations or a radio program and you may not clearly remember getting from one place to another. Your brain and mind are divided between activities.

Compare this coping skill to the God-given "fight or flight" protective response. We have been given the ability to fear. Fear is good within normal limits. We would find ourselves in perilous situations without being alerted to the dangers around us without it. However, fear taken to the extremes of anxiety and panic attacks, phobias and paranoia are counter-productive and do not ultimately protect us.

In the same way, dissociation of ordinary levels is beneficial and allows for a very functional life. Any emotion or characteristic within God's intended parameters is useful. Dissociation within normal levels is good.

However, extremes of dissociation that became necessary for a traumatized child to cope early in life eventually becomes counter-productive later in life. Dissociation is the God-given coping mechanism that allows for the ordinary act separating from the overwhelming memory (this includes body memories, recollection, and the emotions) of a painful event.

Most people who experience the trauma of a traffic accident can describe what happened shortly before and shortly after the impact. Very seldom will someone be able to re-live the exact physical pain or the emotional terror as their vehicle collapsed around them in the collision.

They remember *that* they bled and *that* they experienced horror, but they will not physically feel the flesh sear, the bones crunch, or the intense emotions they had. They might cringe or feel a sensation in their stomachs when thinking about it, but those sensations are not historic body memories or emotional memories.

Those components of memory were dissociated by the natural ability of the brain and the mind to separate from the physical, mental, and emotional pain of the event. If we remembered all our old traumas complete with the physical and emotional parts, life would be very difficult indeed.

For some chronically or acutely traumatized people, dissociation had to be used early and often. Dissociation then became such an effective way of dealing with abuse and trauma that they did not tend to develop or learn other coping mechanisms as they matured.

They did not learn how to process an event. They did not learn how to become assertive. They did not learn to ask for help. They did not learn how to avoid or flee perilous situations. They did not learn to listen to their intuition about certain people, and so on. This becomes a complication later in life when the dissociation begins to break down neurologically and they are left with underdeveloped or undeveloped means to cope and protect themselves.

Components of memory involve the mind, emotions, and the body. As in the example of the traffic accident, the components of memory involving both the body pain and emotional feelings become dissociated to protect from intense pain during the recollection of the event. In this case, there is a partial dissociation because the mind can recall the accident while the other components have been mercifully dissociated by repressing or suppressing or even the use of denial.

Repression, suppression, and denial are found on the normal end of the dissociation continuum. Everyone does this from time to time and thus will have an inkling of a partially Non-Amnesic Dissociation (NAD). If all the components are separated from the event, there would be complete dissociation and the result is amnesia for that event.

Understand that this does not mean that everyone who has been in a severe accident has created an alternate personality or has Dissociative Identity Disorder. It does mean that those who do create multiple personalities are able to develop this natural, God-given ability to protect and cope in the presence of early, extreme, and/or chronic abuse. There will be a more complete discussion of dissociative ability in chapter seven.

3

DEFINITIONS

𝔇efining the nuances of dissociation can be tricky. Language used to describe its essence and characteristics vary from person to person and from professional to non-professional. Each of the definitions below is intended to add to your body of knowledge and give broader understanding to this complex coping mechanism that involves both the physical brain as well as the soul (mind, will, and emotions), and possibly even the spirit of a person.

Dissociation and *disassociation* are both accepted as correct terms. There are authorities who accept the two terms as interchangeable; others make some distinction between them. Splitting, shattering, separating, dividing, fragmenting, and more are some of the informal terms used by survivors to describe their own dissociation.

Association, integration, blending, re-knitting, fusing, and merging are a few terms survivors use to describe the reversal of dissociation. There will be more on this later in chapter fourteen.

The following definitions, principles, and insights about dissociation are from a variety of authors, mental health workers, and counselors. Please note that some of the definitions are from resources that were printed prior to the time that the psychiatric community changed the designation from Multiple Personality Disorder (MPD) to Dissociative Identity Disorder (DID).

These insightful observations are useful to help flesh out the concepts and reinforce common observations about dissociation. The resources listed below would be valuable to obtain for more in-depth study of the subject. They are listed below in random order.

Secret, Don't Tell - the Encyclopedia of Hypnotism by Carla Emery

"Dissociation – any trance state involves some degree of dissociation. Hypnosis is a deliberately induced condition of dissociation. The subject's conscious mind is displaced by some part of his unconscious. Degrees of dissociation correspond to depths of trance."

Conference lecture in Tennessee in 2000 by Dr. Dan Rumberger

"Dissociation – Normal dissociation describes the ability of the brain to do more than one thing at a time. Dissociating is a normal mechanism of the brain to protect. Dissociation is like a submarine with sealed off compartments so the ship does not sink when one compartment is compromised. Traumatic dissociation is the ability of the mind to separate the element of experience from consciousness because no one was present to help process the event.

"Dissociation is a neurological event in the brain. There are two hemispheres in the brain. Sensory input hits the right side of the brain first. The person does not know it until it hits the left side of the brain. It's like the lag between touching a key and seeing an image on the computer screen.

"The brain kicks in adrenaline for the normal fight-or-flight response, but if there is a threat, the right brain kicks out and stores the event differently on the right side and the person does not know that it is there until it gets triggered. Then there may be a flashback."

More than One by Terri A. Clark M.D.

"Dissociation is a defense mechanism that operates unconsciously wherein emotional significance is separated and detached from an idea, situation, or object. In dissociation, it is the ability of the mind to effectively block out the conscious memory and awareness of present events while being preoccupied with other thoughts or mental activities."

Uncovering the Mystery of MPD by James G. Friesen Ph.D.

"Dissociation is the act of defending against pain. It may be the most effective defense people can use, since it is 100% successful. When a person dissociates, he or she separates from the memory of a painful event. When used as a noun, dissociation is a defense mechanism, which is highly successful in forgetting a traumatic event.

"Components, or layers, of dissociation are the mind, the emotions, the body's experience, and the will. One or more of these may be dissociated during a partial dissociation. When all four are dissociated, the amnesia will be total.

"Example: A child goes through a trauma and then pretends to be a new person (alternate personality or alter), to whom those bad things did not happen. There's separation from the memory and it's immediately and completely forgotten. The newly created alter "remembers" only a blank spot where the trauma happened – referred to as time loss. If the dissociation is complete, the amnesia for that event is 100% for that part.

Beyond Tolerable recovery by Ed M. Smith Ph.D.

"Dissociation is the separation that occurs in a person's mind between the conscious and subconscious mind. It's a type of self-defense, protecting from extreme pain or fear. Normal dissociation is experienced in a lesser degree, for example, through daydreaming during stressful or boring situations, or by "highway hypnosis." During extreme pain or fear the child will mentally assign their pain to other created psychodynamic parts of their mind, or alters who carry out specific functions for the child."

How Can I Help? by Alaine Pakkala

"I view MPD as God's gift to prevent insanity in children. The horrendous abuse suffered by those who are ritually abused usually begins before age of 3 or 4. The child, *unable to process* the atrocities she suffers splits off the memory of this abuse into one area of her mind. Later, as abuse continues, more memories are split off and removed from her conscious mind. It is as though the core person has amnesia concerning these events, being unable to recall, at will, what she has gone through."

Multiple Identities by Diane Hawkins

"The phenomenon of dissociation lies on a

continuum, however, that progresses to conditions which become increasingly more pathological and disruptive to normal functioning. Dissociative Identity Disorder is the most extreme form, involving the complete splitting of the soul. Since the soul encompasses the mind, the will, and the emotions of the person, each split-off part will have an independently functioning mind, will, and capacity for emotions."

Diagnostic criteria from the DSM 5

1. Two or more distinct identities or personality states are present, each with its own relatively enduring pattern of perceiving, relating to and thinking about the environment and self. … personality states may be seen as an "experience of possession." These states "involve(s) marked discontinuity in sense of self and sense of agency, accompanied by related alterations in affect, behavior, consciousness, memory, perception, cognition, and/or sensory-motor functioning. These signs and symptoms may be observed by others or reported by the individual.

2. Amnesia must occur, defined as gaps in the recall of everyday events, important personal information and/or traumatic events.

3. The person must be distressed by the disorder or have trouble functioning in one or more major

life areas because of the disorder.

4. The disturbance is not part of normal cultural or religious practices.

5. The symptoms are not due to the direct physiological effects of a substance (such as blackouts or chaotic behavior during alcohol intoxication) or a general medical condition (such as complex partial seizures).

The above briefly conveys the criteria. The DSM-5 invites readers to see their article for expanded definitions and additional signs of DID on their internet site.

More and more professionals, ministers, and counselors are adding to the body of knowledge about Dissociative Identity Disorder. There remain, however, many who continue to totally discount DID as non-existent or assume it is the presence of demons or some other mental illness.

The DSM first listed MPD in 1980. Prior to that, people were diagnosed with schizophrenia, bi-polar, borderline personality, psychoses, neuroses, etc. As previously stated, they were then given medications that corresponded to those diagnoses.

HINT: If someone comes to you having been diagnosed with many different "psycho-labels," you may very well be dealing with unrecognized DID, especially if the person acknowledges early trauma of some kind.

It cannot be emphasized enough that clusters of signs and symptoms must be ascertained and differentials must be accounted for or eliminated to be relatively confident that you are dealing with a person who is DID on some level.

4

TERMINOLOGY

𝕿he following terms come from a variety of sources. Find the terms that are meaningful and use them in your ministry to dissociative people. To reduce confusion, it is prudent to use terms that are universally known and accepted. However, if the dissociative person has his or her own "language" then use that instead. For example, she may prefer to say "blended" rather than integrated.

Abreaction or Flashback – A memory is triggered by one of the senses, a season, an anniversary, or some other cause and re-lived as if it were happening all over again. She may not be in touch with her present circumstances during the abreaction. She may appear to be in a trance and will sense things and say things that are not accurate to her present situation.

Alter, Personality, Part, Persona, Identity – Alternative personality or alternative identity that has been dissociated from the original person. She may have a different name, gender, handwriting, age, and more.

Amnesia – The full or partial absence of memory components by any personality of what the body did while that alter was not in executive control. Amnesia can block one part from knowing what other parts are doing. It is also a factor in causing an alter to believe that she is alone in the system, that is, she is a person without multiple personalities because she is not aware of other parts or the rest of her life events.

Body memory – Physical symptoms (pain, rash, scars, blisters, symptom of an illness, nausea, headache, bruising, shaking, seizure, etc.) from past events may surface in the present when the affected personality switches in during a flashback or when that part takes executive control of the body.

Co-consciousness – The ability of the core or any of the alters to share consciousness with others. It may be mutual between the alters or more like a one-way mirror in which one alter is aware of the other but not vice-versa.

Core Person or birth person or original self or original identity – This is the original person from whom all the alters were formed. No alter has any attribute, trait, or quality which it did not obtain from the original core person.

Dissociative Ability – The ability to dissociate. There are many professionals who believe that some people have brain structure and other genetic factors that make them more able to dissociate than people who do not have it.

Emoter – These alters carry emotions. The personality who is in executive control may not know why she is feeling angry, depressed, afraid, etc. because the emoter alters who have been triggered carry the emotional pain from the memory that has been triggered unknowingly. The alter's emotions may "seep" into the core person, host, or another alter who is currently in executive control who then feels the emoter's strong feelings but has no idea why.

Executive control or out – The personality, host, or core person who is in control of the body speaks, acts, and makes the decisions while in executive control of the body. The host, for example, may lose time and wonder who was "out" based on changes in time, place, clothing, etc. An alter who has been triggered may not have been out since the original trauma that split her off and will be disoriented if she has not been co-conscious with others.

Fragment – An alter which does not have a fully developed personality since it carries a very small segment of the person's life. It may be created in a one-time event, it may have a singular purpose, or the trauma was so extreme that each fragment is only able to bear a few seconds of the memory.

Host – An alter who appears to be the original identity, may have her name, but functions as a part who interacts with people on a "normal" level. This alter may think she is the core person. She will often feel or sense what the other alters do, but without having knowledge of precisely why. She will be in executive control most of the time and reflects the inner world to the outside world and vice-versa.

Integration, fusion, association, blending or re-knitting – This is the opposite of or reversal of dissociation. Integration can occur intentionally after healing or spontaneously when there is significant healing to one or more personalities. Alters can integrate with each other or the core person. With integration comes mutual realization of memories and emotions that were once held separately by the alters.

Observer – These are often child alters generally around the age of three or four. They are able to "travel" within the system and observe or sense what is going on with other alters.

Persecutor – A negative, destructive, sabotaging personality who acts out because of horrible memories, misinformation, programming, and/or demonization. They often think they are protecting the entire system by doing so. ("I must keep her quiet so if I punish that personality, she won't give away our secrets and endanger us by telling.")

Program – A compulsive behavior which the person "must" do when triggered by a stimulus which has been implanted by hypnosis and/or the result of trauma. These may be installed intentionally or be habits which have become deeply ingrained and automatic almost like a superstition taken to extremes.

Protector – All alters protect, but these protect in any way that will keep others from finding out about the dissociation itself or keep others from getting too close to secrets. Protectors will often display anger, anti-social behavior, or acerbic humor and sarcasm. They are generally older alters who protect damaged child alters.

Ritual Abuse – This is usually associated with either witchcraft or Satanism, however, a person would be considered a ritual abuse survivor when her abuse was regular and systematic. It would be like the teenager who was abducted and subjected to constant abuse until her escape or like the child who was molested every time her mother left her alone with her father.

Switch – Change in executive control. Most switching is subtle; however, there is often head, posture, or eye movement that is a clue. Eyes may be directed straight up or to one side, they may close in prolonged blink, or there may be a sigh or a change of body position to try to mask the switch from one personality to another.

System – The sum of the original person and all of the alters. Some internal systems are described by various alters as containing elements that are encountered in the outside world, that is, buildings, forests, cities, etc. in which the various alters live.

Time Loss or amnesia – The core person or any alter may describe their amnesic periods as lost time because another part is in executive control and they are not co-conscious. No actual time is lost because the totality of the core plus alters hold all the time.

5

TYPES OF DISSOCIATION

𝕿here are several types or categories or degrees of dissociation that occur along the dissociation continuum. Identifying them will help you to better define and understand dissociation observed in yourself or others.

All dissociative people used to be lumped into one category. There needs to be a distinction between those who have highly complex alternate personality systems and those who have a less extensive system or no system at all.

By highly complex, I mean those who have hundreds or even thousands of personalities. Those personalities may be amnesic, partially amnesic, have borderline personality traits, and may carry a large or small segment of memories. These highly complex systems are generally found in survivors of ritual abuse and will not be dealt with in this work.

Note: When you encounter someone who has

more than fifty to one hundred personalities, suspect Satanic or Witchcraft ritual abuse.

Reactive DID (RDID)

These people generally have fewer than 50 to 100 alters. The trauma was significant, but not like someone who has endured trauma on the far end of the *severity of abuse continuum*. These will have an "explosion" at the point of trauma during which one or more alters will emerge whose function is to protect the original person from the pain of that memory. This can be compared to a pane of glass dropped onto the floor and fragmenting in a random fashion.

A woman was raised in a home by an angry, alcoholic father and a non-nurturing mother. She was neglected as an infant and molested by her friend's father at age five. She immediately split off several personalities to carry the intense emotions. The little girl's mother did not believe her when she told her what had happened because "she was not upset enough." The mother could not know that the abused child had dissociated her emotions.

By not believing and helping her little girl process the event, the mother reinforced the need to cope by dissociation. If the mother would have believed her, told her that it was not her fault, or called the police, the little girl would have developed coping skills that would serve her well for any subsequent traumas.

Dissociation worked *for* her therefore she continued to split off personalities whenever she encountered traumatic events. Dissociation worked *against* her because her mother thought she should have been more emotional and so her story was dismissed and thus she did not receive the help that she needed.

Intentional DID (IDID)

Highly complex systems of intentionally dissociated individuals are the result of calculated, extreme trauma of an enduring, ritualistic nature. Personalities are also programmed into the system. The purpose of these programmed personalities is protection of the core person as well as to provide a means of control by their programmers. Hypnosis and drugs are often used in conjunction with trauma to accomplish this fragmenting.

Most of these DIDs are the result of Satanic Ritual Abuse (SRA), Witchcraft Ritual Abuse (WRA) and/or Masonic Ritual Abuse (MRA). This can be compared to a pane of glass that has been scored in specific patterns prior to being dropped onto the floor. It results in predictable, controllable fragments as well as some random splits that are not controllable by the abusers.

Non-Amnesic Dissociation (NAD)

These people have distinct personalities who exercise control, but unlike some of the alters of the classic DID systems, these alters are aware of each other, that is, they are co-conscious with each other. These people may be better described as having personality shifts which are based on the emotion carried by each of the parts.

Anger tends to be the most dominant emotion. Normal anger should be experienced as a bell curve. It builds up, peaks, and gradually tapers back down. For the NAD, it will be the same as with any DID with distinct personalities. Anger is at zero, goes straight to ten on a scale of zero to ten, and then drops back to zero again and she goes on as if nothing happened.

These people may never come for counseling for NAD since they generally function well socially, academically, and in the market place. They usually do not recognize the shifts in attitudes and behavior. The NAD would likely not be diagnosed with DID since it is closer to the "normal" end of the *dissociation continuum.*

There are times, however, when an NAD will be baffled when she knows that she is very capable as a rule, but when "triggered" she will feel childlike or inept despite knowing that she knows how to handle the situation. Or she may be critically verbalizing something while thinking, "I don't mean this, why am I saying this? Why can't I shut up?" or "I'm an adult, why do I feel like a child?"

It is as if she were standing back and watching or listening to herself, yet being unable to fully experience or control what she is saying or doing. Some women who have experienced severe Pre-Menstrual Syndrome describe a similar type of thing when they have a hormonally driven "hissy fit." (This does not mean that they are dissociative.)

Traumatic Dissociation (TD)

These people have one or perhaps two dissociated personalities that do not take executive control unless triggered. At that point, they may have a flashback or abreaction. They generally experienced one major trauma. They are generally very functional and need help to deal with the event or events that caused the traumatic dissociation.

Their traumas usually center on a life-threatening disease, the death of a close relative or friend, some severe injury, or a single abusive event. They may come for ministry for other issues because the TD does not usually affect them enough to interfere with their life.

Sometimes there will be vague knowledge of the trauma so that it is as if the person has this knowledge because someone else told her about the event. This variation could be explained by the presence of an alter whose "job" it is to carry that memory. Because of the overwhelming feelings associated with the trauma, that personality "seeps" information and/or emotions to the core person who then has an inkling of the event, but doesn't truly "own" it.

A typical example would be an adult relating the story of his childhood leukemia as if he was giving an account of someone he knows quite well. "There was a little boy who…" and then he concludes the story by saying "… and that little boy was me."

The apostle Paul referred to a traumatic event in which he was left for dead after being stoned. He described it in 2 Corinthians 12: 2 – 6 in the same way as those with traumatic dissociations describe their memories: *"I know a man in Christ who fourteen years ago – whether in the body I do not know, or out of the body I do not know, God knows – such a man was caught up to the third heaven."* He continues his story and then reveals that he was that man. We do not know if Paul was dissociative or not, but it is an interesting passage of Scripture.

Borderline Personality (BP)

Children with low dissociative ability who experience extreme trauma are incapable of dissociating from the memories effectively and cleanly enough to allow them to function in other areas of their lives. There is much distortion of reality. Distortion of memories may also come from having been drugged, hypnotized, or subjected to some cult practices. They may also have a low mental capacity and be incapable of dissociating very well.

Alters with Borderline Personality traits have a surrealistic notion of the past, wondering if it was a memory, a nightmare, or just something made up based on what they have read, heard, or seen in the media. Many of these children are killed by the cults because they may talk about the memory fragments and endanger the cult. Others are found in mental wards or prisons.

Note that Borderline Personality Disorder is a distinct psychological diagnosis. It should also be noted that BPD has its own continuum that ranges from mild to severe.

Normal Dissociation

Normal dissociation allows people to multi-task. It provides the ability to focus on more than one thing at a time. Some people are more adept than others, but everyone has this marvelous God-given skill. Few people have not been caught up in thoughts and been brought back by someone saying, "Hey, where have you been for the last five minutes?" They have been following up on another thought or forming a reply to some point in the conversation. That describes normal dissociation.

Normal dissociation also allows for day-dreaming or fantasy, creativity or imaginary friends. Highway hypnosis, self-induced trances and hypnotism, as well as suppression, repression, and denial would also fall under the general category of normal dissociation *if* it is within normal limits and done to a reasonable extent.

Each of the items in the normal dissociation category has its own continuum. The continuum may vary from occasional fantasizing, for example, to chronic episodes. It can vary from mild to intense. When it borders on the chronic and intense end of the continuum for that type of normal dissociation, there may be more serious underlying issues with which to deal.

6

DISSOCIATION CONTINUUM

𝕴t is useful to think of Dissociative Identity Disorder on a continuum since not all dissociative people are the same. Typically, they will each have different combinations of dissociation.

Dissociation, dissociative ability, and trauma are all related components of DID. Again, not all dissociative people have Dissociative Identity Disorder. Not all of those with DID have the same size system. Dissociation ranges from mild to severe, normal to extreme.

At the top end of the *dissociation continuum* where there has been extreme trauma, there will be survivors of various kinds of ritual abuse. They will typically display combinations of all of the types of dissociation mentioned on the continuum. They will have a predominance of intentionally dissociated parts which have been programmed by a cult or a predator.

At the lower end of the dissociation continuum where there has been minimal trauma or milder but chronic abuse, there will be little or no dissociation other than the God-given capacity to function in mundane tasks. Those who were blessed with someone to help them process a trauma would not have had to resort to dissociation to cope. Still others would have learned better coping skills prior to the trauma and would not have needed to continue to dissociate and/or create new personalities. Others were traumatized past the age at which dissociation can be used.

A child who was subjected to molestation by her father and disbelieved by her mother resorted to dissociation. She created several personalities initially and then more as she encountered other traumas later in life.

Another child subjected to the same level of molestation by a neighbor was believed and cared for physically and emotionally by her parents. She did not dissociate. It was the same type of abuse, but by different people – one was a close relative and the other was a neighbor. There were critical differences in support and processing of the trauma.

In another instance, a woman was dissociative because of childhood sexual abuse. She had a compact system which consisted mainly of wounded child alters and various adult parts who carried out normal functions of mother, wife, homemaker, churchgoer, and other adult functions. One day, she got into a physical altercation with her daughter-in-law and she created a new alter at age sixty-two. She had never learned new coping skills to deal with life's difficulties so she resorted to dissociation once again.

In the middle ranges between Traumatic Dissociation and Normal Dissociation, there will be people who have survived lesser traumas. Perhaps a girl was fondled but not raped. She could still display dissociative traits but would not be considered DID.

Others may have been subjected to sustained chaos, violence in the home, and/or verbal abuse and subsequently resorted to extreme daydream and fantasy to avoid thinking about the abuse. These survivors would also be dissociative but would not be considered DID.

Again, each sub-category has its own continuum. Some people rarely daydream or fantasize while others engage in it extensively to escape from stressful memories. There are more and more people resorting to video and computer games to escape reality. They can become trancelike with many of these activities.

Generally, someone who has been subjected to

fewer and lesser traumas would not have the need to dissociate as much as someone who was subjected to chronic and extreme trauma. Someone whose trauma did not start until age four or five would generally not have as extensive a system as someone whose torture started in the womb.

The following chart summarizes the types of dissociation that have been discussed above. It reflects a typical ascending order of the expected dissociation based on the intensity of the trauma to which the person was subjected.

There will, of course, be many variations in each person's system due to age, type of trauma, personality, gender, support system, ability to process the trauma because of intervention, other coping skills, and so on.

EXTREME TRAUMA

Borderline Personality Disorder

Intentional DID

Reactive DID

Non-Amnesic Dissociation

Traumatic Dissociation

Normal Dissociation

LITTLE OR NO TRAUMA

In summary, when you encounter someone who displays symptoms of dissociation, you are encountering someone who has been traumatized. Ritual abuse of some kind should be suspected after finding over fifty to one hundred alters. Often the DID displays a puzzling combination of traits which are confusing and contradicting. This would likely be complicated by other behavioral, mental, and emotional issues.

Once DID is confirmed, it takes the mystery out of the equation and the behaviors and verbalizations of the person make more sense to you as the observer of a person with puzzling traits. If you are the dissociative one, it helps you understand the inconsistencies in mood, tastes, preferences, and more that may have made you feel like a "crazy" person.

7

DISSOCIATIVE ABILITY

Dissociative Ability is simply the ability of the brain to dissociate. When one encounters an event that is laden with overwhelming emotion, the brain is able to divert the memory components to parts of the brain other than it normally would. Thus, certain memories are unavailable unless triggered in some way.

Brain function is very sophisticated and fascinating, but will not be dealt with in this work other than making some basic observations that relate to dissociation. We will only look at some of the basic memory components.

Components of the same memory are stored in different areas of the brain under normal circumstances. There is muscle/body memory, symbolic/visualized memory, verbal memory, and emotional memory.

Some memory is stored in the right hemisphere of the brain and some memory is stored in the left hemisphere. Complete memory recall includes visual images, sounds/words, senses (what was seen, heard, smelled, tasted, felt, and/or touched), and the associated emotions.

It has been observed that if a mother is dissociative, then her children are more readily able to dissociate. The question is whether the dissociation is a heritable genetic trait or the probability that both the mother and her daughters were traumatized early in life.

There are instances in which a mother who is unstable and switches into different personalities has children who either learn to shift their own personalities to match or counter the mother's changes, or else, they may truly be dissociating and switch into the appropriate personality to cope with the mother.

Dissociative ability also describes the ability of a person's mind, will, and emotions to dissociate. These are soul level issues. There is an element of willful choice that can become a habitual mindset. Dissociative ability also allows for the emotions to be dissociated so that, while there is cognitive recognition of abuse, the emotions are intentionally separated from the memory.

A little girl, accustomed to being beaten whenever she displeased her mother's boyfriend, automatically dissociated in those situations. Her mind would slip away to thoughts and visualizations of being in her biological father's favorite place and being safely with him there. Her dissociative ability allowed her to deal with the actual or anticipated abuse.

Dissociative Ability plus unprocessed trauma results in some level of dissociation. It is useful to try to confirm that you might be working with a dissociative person by looking at these categories to determine the approximate level of dissociative ability (DA). If someone has low DA, then you may be looking at some other condition. Some of these things can be objectively observed by you or reported to you by the person with whom you are working. You may notice them in yourself.

Look for clusters of traits. If a person displays one or two items, no matter how extreme, it may or may not indicate DA that leads to dissociation. However, one or two items may be all that is obvious until more extensive conversations or observations uncover some of the other hidden traits. Remember that part of the function of dissociation is to disguise its very presence.

Be careful not to "diagnose" or jump to any conclusions that are not warranted. Watch for other explanations as well. For example, there are many highly intelligent, creative people who are not dissociative despite their potential for having a high dissociative ability.

Remember, that just because there is moderate or high dissociative ability, it does not necessarily mean that a person has dissociated. It simply means that *if* dissociative ability is present *and* it is coupled with unprocessed early trauma, it is likely that the person would have coped by dissociating. Someone who has dissociative ability but processes the trauma well or has learned other strong coping skills may not dissociate at all.

You may also be observing one personality or several without knowing it. Be aware that the host personality may be in executive control for most of the time that you are observing her because *your* presence triggers her presence and therefore your conclusions would be based on her character alone. You may then be bewildered by her sharp recall during one session and total lack of it in another if you do not detect any switch in personalities.

Note also that Dissociative Ability has its own continuum. There are those who have very high DA and those who have low DA as well as those in-between. Each alter may have a different level of dissociative ability. That phenomenon is demonstrated more clearly in the survivors at the far end of the abuse continuum.

Generally, the more traits that are seen, the more likelihood of higher DA. Again, each of the DA traits has its own continuum. Many of the following statements are true about those with DA and dissociation on some level:

1. Females have a higher DA than males because of the structure of the brain.

2. Children display results of higher DA than adults. An adult will not usually create new alters like a child would.

3. Despite low scoring in IQ tests or other evaluations of mental function for some, these are generally highly intelligent people. Their brains had to work very hard to keep them safe.

4. She uses that IQ in creative outlets such as art, music, drama, or writing and especially poetry.

5. She may use self-hypnosis and can become trance-like at times using a mirror, staring, playing computer games, etc.

6. She is very susceptible to suggestion.

7. She is usually very visual with a vivid imagination and inventiveness.

8. She had an imaginary friend as a child.

Again, it is important to look for clusters of traits as well as the extent of the traits that indicates the level of dissociative ability.

The above traits and characteristics are observable especially in a consistent personal or professional relationship which provides an opportunity for the detection of clusters of dissociation characteristics.

It is important to look for differentials, that is, other explanations for the attribute. An only child may create an invisible friend out of loneliness. Self-hypnosis may have been a game that the child's dissociative friend or the media taught her or that she stumbled upon on her own. Creativity and intelligence may have been inherited and not "amplified" because the child needed to find creative ways to stay safe and develop intelligent means to outwit a predator.

If we were to make a graphical correlation between a person's Dissociative Ability and the Intensity of Abuse that she endured, we could make general conclusions about the type and size of system the person would likely have developed. Knowing approximately where a person falls in the graph can help you evaluate how dissociated or fragmented she is likely to be.

There would be clues to degrees of amnesia. You would be able to observe levels of co-consciousness and will better be able to minister to her. If she knows that you understand, she will be more likely to continue to be transparent and trusting.

A woman who spent most of her adult years in counseling confessed, "I never opened up because I knew that they didn't know how to help me." The more you understand, the more your counselee is likely to let you in.

Two other factors are pertinent to the discussion. They are not reflections of dissociative ability, rather they are important markers in dissociation. Their presence or absence help to determine the presence of some level of dissociation.

Amnesia is one of the key issues in uncovering dissociation and dissociative ability. Since memory has several components, it is likely that even "normal" memory will miss one or more of those components. When all of the components are missing, or perhaps misfiled in the brain and mind, there will be complete amnesia for the event. Amnesia can be partial. Memory can also be distorted because of poor dissociative ability, drugs, programming, and/or hypnosis.

Co-consciousness is another pertinent matter related to dissociation and the dissociative ability of a person. It describes the ability of one alter to be conscious of the memories, activities, and emotions of another alternate personality.

There are differing levels of co-consciousness. Some personalities are mutually fully conscious of other ones. Some personalities know of the host and a few others but are unaware of any others. Some will know some things about other parts, but not everything. Some personalities know other personalities, but like a one-way mirror, it is not mutual. There are other personalities who have no awareness of anyone else and are totally isolated within the system.

Looking below in the chart at representative examples, Child X with high DA who was subjected to occasional molestation by her older brother would likely have some RDID or perhaps a TD. She may or may not have amnesia for the events. She may or may not have a distinct personality who handled the abuse. She may be NAD.

Child Y with low DA subjected to the same molestation would more likely have some distortion or even BP.

Child Z with moderate DA and extreme trauma would be expected to have all types of dissociation and combinations of amnesia and co-consciousness.

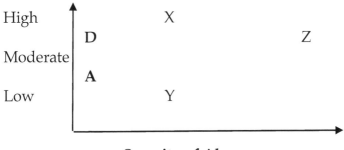

Severity of Abuse
(No trauma - moderate/chronic - acute/constant)

In summary, there are differing types of dissociation, differing types of amnesia, and differing levels of co-consciousness combined with dissociative ability.

Each dissociative person has her own cluster of symptoms and indicators. Different intelligence, creativity, gender, personality, age, birth order, family, culture, and socio-economic factors determine the system that emerges within each person.

The following is a quick list of the types of dissociation, types of amnesia, and levels of co-consciousness for your review:

Types of Dissociation

BP   Borderline Personality Disorder
IDID   Intentional DID
RDID   Reactive DID
NAD   Non-Amnesic Dissociation
TD   Traumatic Dissociation
Normal No Dissociation

Types of Amnesia

Full Amnesia
Partial Amnesia
No Amnesia
Distortion

Co-consciousness

Full
Partial
"One-way mirror"
None

The following are general principles about the above Dissociative Ability/Severity of Abuse graph:

1. Everyone has some level of dissociative ability and can be placed along the *dissociative ability continuum* from low to high.

2. Everyone can be placed along the *severity of abuse*

continuum from none to extensive.

3. There are an infinite number of dissociation configurations possible based on dissociative ability, abuse, amnesia, and co-consciousness.

4. The same abuse experienced at the same age by the same perpetrator will result in different configurations in each victim because of variations in personality, temperament, gender, support, birth order, other experiences, other coping skills, etc.

5. The better the processing of trauma and/or abuse at its occurrence, the less damage will be incurred. Processing is ideal when it comes from an affirming adult bringing immediate intervention to the child.

6. The more severe and frequent the abuse or trauma, the more fragmentation is probable.

7. The higher the dissociative ability, the more fragmentation is probable.

8. The lower the dissociative ability, the higher the probability of memory distortion and/or borderline personality traits.

9. Distortion may also be the product of intentional programming or hypnosis in Ritual Abuse or diminished mental function because of retardation

or traumatic injury which is the cause of some organic brain damage in the individual.

10.   There can be a wide range of amnesia within the partial amnesia designation from just having inklings to having a majority of the information, sensory data, and/or emotions related to a particular event.

8

DISTINCTIONS BETWEEN ALTERS AND DEMONS

𝕿rauma and abuse are the result of sin which entered the world with the fall of Adam and Eve. Acts of sin as well as the presence of sin can create strongholds in a person's life. Demons inhabit strongholds. They are the vantage points from which demons oppress.

The Greek word for stronghold, *topos*, was a military term from which we get our word topography. It describes a place or a strategic position from which an enemy can attack. Sin, whether by or against someone, generates a stronghold which produces the position from which a demon may oppress. The demon is given its so-called legal right to oppress a person because of the sin.

Satan and his minions are legalists and squatters. Satan is like a lion who seeks to kill, steal, and destroy. Like a natural lion, a demon will go after the unprotected, the young, the wounded, and the stragglers. We scream in protest that it is not fair that the victim is not only subjected to abuse, but is also subjected to a demonic oppressor if the event is not addressed in a way that also takes care of spiritual issues.

It does not matter whether a person is dissociated or not. If a person is dissociated, the demon will likely oppress one individual part while other parts are unaffected by that particular demon. If a person is not dissociated, and is subjected to sin, she can also have strongholds created in her life from which demons oppress.

There are far too many horror stories told by dissociative people who have sought help from the Church. They have been told that there is no such thing as multiple personalities; therefore, the appearance of an alter is demonic and it must be cast out. Several dissociative people have reported faking a deliverance just to get out of the clutches of the well-meaning, but inexperienced church people.

Think of the apostle Paul who was thwarted by Satan, who had a thorn in the flesh, a messenger of Satan. If he could be plagued and tormented by a demon, then we are not exempt.

Abuse and trauma survivors are just as

susceptible to being oppressed by a demon as any other believer. Dissociative and non-dissociative believers are equally vulnerable to demonic attack.

Please note that the Greek New Testament word, daimonizomai, should be more accurately transliterated as "demonized" rather than "possessed" as it is often translated.

An unbeliever can be possessed, that is, controlled by a demon. A believer can be afflicted physically, emotionally, or mentally, but the demon would not occupy the spirit of a person who is a believer and has the Holy Spirit according to several passages of Scripture.

Occasionally a person will have a full blown demonic manifestation. The demon may take over all mental and bodily functions or just some aspect. The following is a list of some of the demonic manifestations that may occur:

Headache
Dizziness
Pressure – usually in the chest
Choking sensation, gagging
Bizarre or foreign thoughts suddenly appear
Strong emotions suddenly appear
Sudden attitude change: arrogant, uncooperative, defensive, hostile, etc.
Restlessness

Inability to concentrate

Altered senses: deaf, mute, blind, and/or sensory changes (pain, burning, numbness, etc.)

Nausea, queasiness, vomiting

Seizure

Self-destructive behavior: head banging, hitting self, cutting, scratching/gouging, hair pulling, use of razors or knives, etc.

Whenever a demon manifests, it is not in its so-called assigned place. A full-blown manifestation is the last desperate measure a demon will use to try to intimidate and maintain its place.

The following are some of the key differences between an alternate personality and a demon.

Alter	Demon
Alters can be integrated but cannot be cast out.	Demons can be cast out.
Alters will initially appear out of sync with the person but will gradually move into harmony and	The demon remains distinct and distant. Healing will not change its personality or make

change with healing.	it conform to that of the person.
Confusion, fear, and other negative emotions decrease with effective healing in an alter.	Demons weaken in power but not in character. Emotions they produce remain consistent, but not as strong.
Alters may have voices distinct from the core person, but it will be consistent with its host and it will definitely be human in character.	A demon may manifest with a voice that imitates the person or it may be raspy or abrasive with hissing or other non-human sounds.
An alter may express strong emotions but will soften with healing and deliverance.	A demon's character and/or assignment will not change so anger, hatred, etc. remain.
The imagery of an alter is human in form even if it is not identical with the body's size, gender, age, etc.	Demons can shift from human to non-human form with many variations.
The alter will be truthful and correct any errors after healing.	Demons will try to lie, mislead and seek to deceive within the parameters set.

The alters' purpose is to protect the core person from pain. They are not generally destructive unless under the influence of a demon or programmed to be so. They will respond to healing and protect in a more positive manner.	Demons are destructive in nature and purpose. The last thing they want is to manifest. They prefer deceiving their "host" into believing that they are part of their personality, just an undisciplined emotion, that they have a right to be there, or that they are a friend.
Alters generally fall into sub-categories and can be classified by their human characteristics.	Demons may try to manifest as an alter (pseudo-alter).

9

RECOGNIZING DISSOCIATION

$\mathfrak{A}$gain, one of the highest priorities of the dissociative person, no matter where they fall on the continuum, is to mask the very presence of their dissociation. Many dissociaters feel a sense of shame or embarrassment about being dissociative. This seems to be especially true if there are distinct personalities present within a complex system.

She will often be secretive about her life. She may answer direct questions with vague replies that are meaningless. She may misdirect the entire conversation with "rabbit trails." She will often be evasive about her past and present experiences and circumstances. Sometimes this is because she genuinely does not know and feels compelled to make something up that is consistent with what she does happen to know.

Some of the characteristics common to dissociative people could describe anyone who has endured trauma but did not dissociate. Each quality has its own continuum from mild and hardly noticeable to intense and dominating.

You may encounter someone who is merely ambivalent. Ambivalence is at one end of the continuum, equal and opposite feelings and statements are at the other end and likely to be evidence of some level of dissociation if clustered with other dissociation traits.

Ambivalence is common in a world that offers many choices. She feels one way at one moment and then changes her mind. Does she just have a problem making up her mind? Is she an extreme people-pleaser or are different personalities expressing opposing views?

Are sleep disturbances because of DID or perhaps depression or another condition or a medication? Is she experiencing time losses or is she forgetful because of a chaotic life or perhaps from an old brain injury? Does she have trouble with time management because of an attention deficit disorder or is there a lot of switching which makes it difficult for her to keep track of time?

If a person presents with a physical symptom, like a rash, it must be determined if it came from an allergy, poison ivy, or impetigo. In the same way, always look for and explore differentials, that is, differing reasons that might be responsible for the symptom or behavior.

The following characteristics and clues are not exhaustive. They must be considered in context of the person's whole life. These characteristics must also be considered as having continuums from mild to extreme. Not all dissociaters have all the characteristics. Again, look for clusters of characteristics and differentials before dissociation and/or DID should be considered.

The following are also generalities. There are exceptions which can make it more difficult to recognize the presence of dissociation. Again, be aware that traits and characteristics may be intentionally masked or minimized to disguise the presence of DID.

1. Time loss. She may readily admit "lost time" of seconds, minutes, hours, days, or even years. She may or may not be aware of the time losses. She may report that she suddenly finds herself in a different setting and wearing different clothing hours or days later without knowing what happened in the interim. She may state that there is no recollection of early years. Most people will have at least some memories prior to age 5. There may be whole years missing. She may also deny an action that you clearly witnessed because some other part did it during the host's time loss.

2. There has been a significant trauma, usually sexual, before age 5 to 7. This event will produce an intolerable conflict between what is and what should be. That intolerable conflict makes dissociation necessary. (My daddy hurt me – my daddy loves and protects me.)

3. She makes equal and opposite statements, disjointed sentences, jumps from subject to subject in a short amount of time and sometimes in the same breath. Therefore, *you* feel confused and uncertain because of her certainty.

4. She may make odd statements such as "If someone notices me, I know people can see me." "I have no substance." "I can't move myself, but someone else can." "I want to be a real person." "I saw myself from above do or say _____." "I've never been 33." (And she is 33!) "I eat food but sometimes 'I' can't taste it." "My body (arm, leg, finger) moves but I don't move it."

5. She may speak of herself in the plural. "We just got back from the store." (And you know that she went alone.)

6. Dissociative people are very spiritually gifted and discerning. They consistently report seeing and hearing things in the spiritual realm. Be aware that there may be counterfeit gifts that must be renounced, especially in those who have been

subjected to Satanists or WICCANS.

7. For those with distinct personalities in an organized system, she will, with trust, refer to herself in a way that includes her system. For example, Jane & Associates, Jane & Troops, Jane & Family, Jane & Company, Jane & the Little Rascals, Jane & Gang, Jane, etc., Jane & the Group, Jane & the Little People, Jane & the System, Jane & Committee, or Team Jane.

8. She is highly intelligent and creative. However, when tested she may score very low and function in life very well, or score very high and function very low. It all depends on who takes the test. Often a child alter will be thrust into the stressful test situation and reflect the undeveloped intellect and limited knowledge.

9. More females than males are dissociative. Males generally tend to develop protective coping skills and thus do not dissociate. Those subjected to intentional trauma of ritual abuse will dissociate.

10. DIDs have "hair-trigger" rejection buttons. She may constantly reject others because she believes that others will or have or might reject her. She may react because her counselor is going on vacation and she perceives it as a personal rejection. This is also a BP trait.

11. She may have physical symptoms which give false negative or false positive medical results when she is tested. She will go to the emergency room more often than the average person because of the sudden onset of severe symptoms which are often surfacing body memories.

12. She has a tremendous need to please and to be acceptable to everyone she meets.

13. Rheumatoid arthritis, fibromyalgia, and chronic fatigue syndrome are common ailments. These conditions are consistently found in those with early and chronic trauma. Not everyone with these diseases are dissociative since these conditions have roots in other causes as well.

14. She may have a personality with an eating disorder, or one who is a cutter, a smoker, a curser, or a drinker while the host does not engage in these things and is appalled by the behavior and attitudes of the others.

15. She may have both male and female personalities. Alters' genders have little to do with sex unless programmed for that purpose. Quite often there are male protectors, female emoters, and child observers and/or victims who carry the painful memories.

16. She may have received many psychiatric

diagnoses over the course of her life and she will have many medications for those conditions as well as for other physical ailments.

17. She may suffer from sudden headaches or dizziness during sessions because of switching from one personality to another. Sometimes it is described as dizziness or the head swirling around or some other physical sensation accompanied by indications of specific places on the head – most often the right side. This reflects activity of the alters who have been triggered.

18. She often will not use her given name. She will often despise the original person and thus, hate her name, and will go by her middle name or adopt a completely different name. She may use different names for each part and have different "moods" to go with each name. She may refer to a personality descriptively as "the one who has been peeking around the corner" or "she's my nine-year-old self." One woman had a personality with an attitude who wore a "go-to-hell" hat.

19. She will often have an inordinate need to give many details and to follow every "rabbit trail" when telling you something urgent and will resent deeply any effort on your part to "get to the bottom line" to resolve the issue.

20. Because of difficulties with time and time

management, she likely will feel the need to have a watch with a minimum of date and time functions. Alarms, timers, etc. are even better. Time may be discontinuous and she could have difficulty determining the timing of events. Did it happen yesterday or last week? Did this happen before or after that happened? She may also have difficulty judging how long it may take to complete a task or to drive from one destination to another.

21. Some alters may not have been "out" for years or decades. When triggered to emerge and assume executive control, she will be disoriented and will need to cover for her lack of knowledge within her current situation. The alter may not know about microwaves because she never had one or be mystified by the latest style of her favorite soft drink because the pop top changed since the last time she was out.

22. Alters often despise the original core part for having been weak, little, or vulnerable. They blame the core or little ones for their current situation, yet they may not want to give up their perceived autonomy, get healed, and integrate to strengthen the whole.

23. She may battle suicidal and self-inflicted pain thoughts. She may have attempted suicide and been frustrated by her inability to overdose with drugs or alcohol. Apparently, the toxins are either

dispersed throughout the system or held by one part so it does not affect the whole. Many do not have hangovers. Others may be constantly cut, hurt, sprained, strained, sick, etc. Sometimes it is attention-getting behavior, sometimes it is a result of programming.

24. Blanking out. When trying to process some memories, feelings, etc. she may describe a BLANK or NOTHING or a WALL when she was just there in a memory. It is more than forgetfulness or distraction. It may be demonic interference, but if it persists after prayer, it is likely a protector who does not think that she should know or tell what happened because of a real or imagined threat.

25. Little or no affect (appropriate body language, facial expression, etc.) when describing a memory or present situation. She may state that she can remember the incident, but does not feel anything emotionally. It is as if she is giving a narrative about someone else. This may be because of a traumatic dissociation or because she has dissociated her emotions.

26. Out of body experiences. She may report having watched herself do something from a distant vantage point such as the corner of the room or the top of the lamp. She may say that she observes herself saying or doing something but cannot control what she is saying or doing. This may

reflect a Non-Amnesic Dissociation or it may be one personality being partially co-conscious with those who "own" the memory.

27. Significant teen or early adult trauma, especially sexual, such as rape or marriage to an abusive person. She may report a series of abusive relationships. Rarely will trauma at those ages be the first significant sexual trauma; suspect dissociation, especially if coupled with time loss during early years. She will usually deny early sexual trauma because the memory has been repressed or dissociated.

28. Mannerisms, voice (tone, quality, volume), appearance, posture, hairstyle, vocabulary, handwriting, size, wrinkles, scars, behavior, speech, poise, facial expression, body language, etc. change. These can differ significantly from alter to alter or be very subtle and hardly noticeable changes.

29. Post-Traumatic Stress Disorder. She may display many symptoms of PTSD: flashbacks, night terrors, panic or anxiety, hypersensitive startle response, avoidance, etc. Since she has suffered early trauma, it would naturally follow that she would suffer from PTSD symptoms as well.

30. Pseudo-seizures caused by demonic activity or possibly programming. Some have actual, documented seizures caused by head trauma or

near-death experiences which are not related to the above. This is usually seen in satanic or witchcraft ritual abuse survivors.

31. "All or nothing" emotions. Rather than a gradual rise, peak, and fall, her triggered emotion will go from none to peak and back as opposed to a normal bell curve.

32. She may be on disability for psychiatric or medical reasons. This is typical for those with many diagnoses as well as those with false positive and false negative medical testing.

33. She may be on welfare or be very self-sufficient and functional as a wife, mother, employee, student, etc. Her ability to function may or may not reflect where she falls on the dissociation continuum.

34. She may prefer to play with children rather than interact with other adults. She may be told by others that she acts childlike, especially when she is around children. She may want nothing at all to do with children since they remind her of her own childhood and she cannot bear seeing their perceived vulnerability.

35. Evidence of internal dialogue. She will either report hearing a conversation or words, or she will appear to be listening to internal dialogue during conversations with you. She may speak out loud

and express one or both sides of an internal conversation especially if she believes that no one else is listening.

36. Flashback/abreaction. When triggered, it is as if she is reliving a traumatic experience. She may lose touch with her present physical surroundings. (This would be the one time I would inform her that I will touch her knee or shoulder and then do so gently. This touch brings her back to the present and opens up an opportunity for healing of the alter who has the memory.)

38. History of sleep disturbances. She will report nightmares, night terrors, insomnia, or even too much sleeping.

39. Uneven achievement in school (from year to year, or subject to subject), athletics, other skills and crafts, knowledge, or artistic abilities. She may display her accomplishment at one time and not be able to at another.

40. Difficulty finding parked car. One personality drives, another one shops and does not know where the car was parked. This is more than just forgetfulness or disorientation from being in a large or unfamiliar shopping center.

41. Indecision about which clothes to wear. There may be disagreement between male and female

alters, different ages, sizes, aversions to certain colors or styles, etc. that must be negotiated.

42. Unexplained possessions. One personality may shop or receive or steal something and hide it from the others.

43. Denial of actions clearly observed by others. An alter switches in, says or does something, switches out and leaves the host "holding the bag" and being accused of being a liar.

44. "Mistaken identity" experiences. Different alters with different names may unexpectedly be confronted by someone who knows her in a different context (church, work, neighborhood, store, etc.). Being in the different locations will trigger different personalities to switch into executive control.

45. A general urgency about life as well as for specific projects, including the healing process. Yet, she will also protest that it is going too fast and she reports that she is having difficulty handling the changes and integrations.

46. She will often be able to self-anesthetize from physical pain but she will claim a high pain threshold or deny the pain. It is more likely that a different personality is taking care of the pain.

47. A sense of deprivation and having been "ripped off" most of her life.

48. She is accused of lying or she may admit that she likes to lie. Sometimes she covers up for herself because she is unsure of the truth or facts.

49. She may report looking in a mirror and not recognizing herself. She may report that her hair, complexion, or other physical feature is a different shape or color.

50. She is mystified about how she knows how to do something that she has never done before.

51. She may make statements that make it easy to either recognize or make you start to look at the possibility of dissociation. "I'm not quite lined up." "I feel split." "I feel like a separate person." "There are two of me." "I'm just a kid; I shouldn't be living on my own." "I freaked out a guy I dated because the clothes I wore on the first date weren't anything like the second one. He didn't recognize me at first." "Sometimes I don't know who I am."

There are many variations on the above descriptions due to the person's ability to explain their personal mysteries. There are many who will not admit to some of these items. Some have never been asked pointed questions about DID. Some have never been observed by someone who is familiar with clusters of DID traits and is able to recognize the dissociation.

<u>Caution</u>: If you suspect DID and the person seems unaware of the dissociation, be very careful in how you broach the subject as it can be very alarming to learn this. There are others, however, who finally see their own dissociation and feel relief because dissociation explains so much of their mysterious attitudes and behaviors. She will say, "That makes my life make sense!"

10

SWITCHING

Changing executive control of the body – which includes the mind, will, and emotions of the personality who comes into control – is called switching. How she switches and evidence of the presence of a new personality switching in takes careful observation.

You might think of it as a glove which is being worn by different hands. Each unique hand has its own diverse characteristics so the "glove" acts differently depending upon which hand is moving the glove.

Some people will give very little indication that there has been a switch. It will be obvious in others. Each person will have her own characteristic way of switching and may or may not be aware of the process in herself.

Sometimes the actual switch is missed because of its subtlety or because of a distraction. In that case, one must rely on the evidence of the switch such as a new topic or different body language.

One woman generally just casually crossed or uncrossed her legs when she switched. Her movement was as normal an activity as any non-dissociative person would display. Her switching was confirmed by keen observations by a counselor who noted that it coincided with other changes such as an abrupt shift in subject matter and the quality of her voice.

It was obvious with an older woman with limited movement due to her fibromyalgia and arthritis. Her child alters would switch in and sit cross-legged on the floor when they were the subject of certain memories. They would subsequently be healed and integrated. The adult would switch back in and could not physically manage to get off the floor until a child personality switched back in and got her back on the couch.

The following are some of the most commonly observed switching phenomena and may occur alone or in combination with the others. Remember to account for other legitimate differentials which could explain what is being observed at the time. The switch could be a seamless flow from one alter to another or it could be an abrupt and unmistakable switch in personalities.

THE SWITCH

Eye movement

In the classic eye movement, she will look straight up as if her eyes were rolling back into her head and when the eyes come back down, another personality is present.

There may be glances to the side or downward. Blinking or fluttering, rolling or closing the eyes are also common. She may momentarily stare almost trancelike at a focal point. Each person will consistently display the same eye movement with each switch.

Posture changes

She may shift in a very subtle posture change or use an ordinary movement such as crossing or uncrossing her arms or legs, or have a very noticeable movement such as standing up, sitting on the floor, or slouching in the chair.

She may lower her chin or jut it out more. She may tilt her head to one side or the other. Her shoulders may be thrown back rigidly or she may curl them forward as if to cover or minimize her breasts. She may turn away or face you directly.

<u>Breath</u>

Some have been known to sigh when switching. Others may yawn, sniff, clear their throats, cough, or even sneeze.

Note: In ministry sessions where prayer is used, it is prudent to "watch and pray" since switching often occurs during the prayer.

EVIDENCE OF THE SWITCH

There are other evidences of different alters switching in and out of executive control. The following describe a variety of the typical changes that can occur. Be aware that some dissociative people nearer the normal end of the continuum may not exhibit any external changes at all.

Those with NAD will likely not give much external evidence of switching. Those with TD will not usually switch into the traumatized part unless there has been a significant trigger which might cause an abreaction or flashback.

For some dissociative people, the host or core personality will remain in executive control and she will act as a liaison between the internal world and the external world. There will be little or no external change evident since she will only be reflecting what she is hearing or sensing from internal parts. Be on the alert for subtle changes in the eyes, voice, emotions, subject matter, and mannerisms which reveal the internal part's issues.

Again, remember that one of the major goals of a dissociative person is to disguise or minimize any evidence of DID. Some are very skilled at switching so that even experienced counselors can be fooled.

Generally, the further toward the extreme end of the dissociation continuum a person is, the more clearly evidence of switching and the presence of another personality is. This will also give you an idea of how extensive her system might be.

Again, the following are generalities and all of the items may not apply to everyone.

Facial appearance

Child alters' faces may soften and become rounder without the wrinkles that adult personalities have.

Males will have a "harder" look than females, especially in the jaw line.

Male personalities in females may even appear to have a "five o'clock shadow" or more noticeable facial hair.

There may be differences in facial features, such as how the mouth appears (fuller lips, wider lips, deeper frown, etc.) or variations in the appearance of their eyes (rounder, more slanted, squinting, etc.), skin tone, and more.

In some cases, childhood photographs show such vast differences that it may not look like the same child even when the pictures were taken in the same time period.

Voice

Tone, volume, and quality of the voice often change to reflect the age and gender of the alter. It will also indicate the intensity of the emotions of the different personalities.

A child alter may speak with a lisp or use the "W" sound for the "R" sound as she did when she was a toddler.

Voice changes are more than the normal and expected changes because of mood or the reflection of her intensity of her emotions with regards to a particular event or memory.

Physical ability

There are differences in strength, flexibility, coordination, and stamina. Some personalities are affected by fibromyalgia, for instance, while others are not. Child alters sit in positions that the adult personalities find uncomfortable.

Health differences

One personality may be diabetic with elevated sugar, the rest test normally when they are in executive control.

Arthritis, fibromyalgia, or other debilitating conditions may be isolated in one or several alters but not all of them.

One may have a chronic cough or allergy symptoms and the others do not.

Some smoke and others do not. Other personal habits may not be shared throughout the system.

Handwriting differences

Child alters usually print. Slight or vast variations are common with the adults. Often there will be several different hand-writings within the same letter or document as different personalities contribute to the work.

Several DID counselees corresponded with their counselor using emails. Each personality that contributed to the message used a different style, a different size, and/or a different color of text.

Right-handed/left-handed

Right or left dominance may change between alters. They appear to be ambidextrous, but it is more likely the difference in personalities.

Note that not all ambidextrous people are necessarily dissociative.

Clothing preferences

There seem to be two extremes. It seems to depend upon the gender makeup of the different personalities and/or the need to simplify and reduce conflict. If there are more males than females in the system, their clothing choices will likely reflect it.

There are those who wear a wide variety of styles and colors. One woman had a group of alters who only wore red because of their function. Others only wore blue because they were sad. They had different issues. Still others wore random clothing which did not reflect issues.

The other extreme of "unisex" type clothes (jeans and t-shirts) is used to eliminate conflict between personalities and/or to disguise the switches between male and female alters.

A child may switch in and kick off her shoes or

remove glasses because that is what she did at that chronological age.

Physical size and weight changes

She may wear size ten one day and must wear a size sixteen the next. Dramatic fluctuations in weight and size can occur in a short amount of time.

Grooming and accessories

There may be several different hair styles reflected from adult styles to pony-tails. Watch for a change in hair style with a switch. (Removing a pony-tail, putting hair up into a bun, removing or adding a scarf or clasp, etc.)

Make-up might be worn by an adult or by seductive female personalities. Male alters who switch in after lipstick is applied by female personalities might wipe it off. Others do not wear any makeup as a part of a unisex look.

Jewelry changes and preferences can also indicate the presence of different personalities. It does seem that they all prefer to wear a watch.
Visual acuity

Some need glasses; others do not. If she did not need glasses until she was a teenager, then the pre-teens would likely remove the glasses to see clearly.

Acuity may change temporarily with integration, especially if child alters with no vision issues integrate into an adult who does need glasses.

Vocabulary

There may be some who use a crude vocabulary and others are more refined.

Some sound educated while others may use words of a child or an uneducated person.

The subject matter would likely change with each different personality. Switches between different personalities may be more difficult to detect if the switch is not accompanied by some other evidence of switching.

Intellectual capacity

The age of the alter often reflects changes in the intellectual capacity. There are some alters who have a diminished IQ because of borderline personality issues or they may simply be young and uneducated alters.

It is also common for an alter who claims to be three or four to display more sense and intellect than many adult personalities. Either extreme can show up with dissociation.

Knowledge

Some alters have knowledge and understanding about society, their life in general, and have access to normal bodies of knowledge that would be appropriate to the chronological age of the original person. They would have co-consciousness.

Some personalities have been shut down or hidden inside and have not been co-conscious with others who have kept up with changes in personal circumstances and in society in general. They are not oriented to time (day, month, year), current events (current president, death of close family member, etc.) and they are shocked and disoriented by the information.

Multi-tasking

They can multi-task to a greater degree than most people. It is beyond being ambidextrous. One woman could run two cash registers with two different customers simultaneously. She reported, "It really freaked them out so I don't do that now."

Other physical changes

There can be startling physical differences between one personality and the others which are visible when they switch in and display amazing changes such as alignment of teeth, skin tone, scars, wrinkles, birthmarks, deformities, posture, and so on. These changes are often associated with the body memories of each individual personality.

11

SYSTEMS

𝕿he total of the original person plus all the alternate personalities is called a system. The internal world of the dissociative person on the complex end of the dissociation continuum is organized into a system of personalities who may or may not "inhabit" the internal structures that they visualize and in which they operate.

Those internal structures have been constructed by the dissociative person for various reasons. One is that the structure resembles some actual external structure (building, communication tower, tunnel, etc.) that has significance to the person. Another reason may be that the structure was suggested to her during a hypnotic trance. Sometimes the personalities construct something that gives them a sense of safety and seclusion.

If a person has one or two traumatic dissociations or has Non-Amnesic Dissociation, there will likely not be a distinct, structured internal system. When there are greater numbers of distinct personalities who are organized into various sized groups, there will be a more organized system developed. Most dissociative people will fall somewhere between these two extremes.

As noted in the section on Dissociative Ability, the amount and intensity of trauma an individual is subjected to determines how much fragmenting will occur. Those on the farther end of the abuse continuum will likely develop a distinct system of alters who are organized in a way that is significant to them. As noted previously, she may refer to her system as her associates, troops, family, company, little rascals, gang, group, little people, committee, and so on.

She will describe internal structures and places that could be just like anything in the natural world such as buildings or forests. She may also have descriptions that are mystical and almost like a fairy tale such as tunnels and mazes. Imagery may have been taken from story books or television programs or reality.

Always bear in mind that this is her reality. It is what she constructed to feel safe or has familiarity with and it has become a comfort zone of sorts. It may also be something that was programmed into the ritual abuse survivors. However, even with programming, they always seem to find a way to work out secret places of which their programmers are unaware.

Internal constructions generally correspond with the responsibilities, function, and experiences of the alters. In one woman's system, the protectors wore military gear. In another system, there were houses where the older protectors took care of the younger wounded ones.

A teen described various child alters with no connection between the alters, no structure, very little co-consciousness, and no hierarchy evident. She was, however, aware of the functions of each one. She could tell when Tattoo had been out, for example, because her arms would be covered with childish ink drawings when she came home from school. Another was called Red because she only wore red clothing. Other young alters switched in and got her in trouble for staring or thumb-sucking while she was in school.

Another woman had fewer than thirty personalities in her system. She had some who only wore red and were energetic and upbeat adults. The group that wore only blue were pessimists. The teens wore baggy clothes. Some of the alters had names and she knew their ages, others of different ages did not have names.

A young man had about fifty alters. They were loosely grouped by the age at which he sustained abuse. He did not have names for all of them, only ages, memories, and function. Baggage Handler handled weighty issues. Several of them were named Eight. It was a very bad year for him as evidenced by the number of personalities who were eight years old.

A boy created a system that was much like a video game. They were all females because in his mind, what happened to him by abusive males should not be done to a boy. There were good and bad alters. He had a rule that whenever a good part was created, a demon would come with her. There was a "Devil's formula" that warred against the "Jesus formula." He created new potions and alters daily to deal with his every day stressors.

In the extreme systems that are the result of ritual abuse, there will be more distinct internal structures such as buildings, rooms, cities, woods, tunnels, mazes, towers, out of body places, castles, dungeons, pits, etc.

Working with the system can be challenging when each personality or each group has its own agenda. It is as if they each have blinders on and have a narrow focus because they are not fully co-conscious. They may not understand how they fit with the whole. There may need to be some negotiations to get alters or groups of them to cooperate for the greater good of the whole.

One woman battled with some personalities who were not interested in health issues. She had an internal bargaining session with everyone and reached a deal. She reported, "Everyone inside has agreed to take my vitamins. It took some negotiation, but hey, it's a start."

The various alters within the system will often look different than the adult person seated in front of you to the others within the system. Often the children will look as the person did at a given age. Some personalities are described as taller or thinner, younger or older, having longer or shorter hair, or have other features that are different than the host.

Alters may wear clothing, uniforms, or wield weapons that the others do not. One woman had a fierce male protector who was described as being a foot taller than the body actually was and carried an AK-47. She rationalized, "If I need to create a protector, it might as well be a big, strong guy."

Many alters will have various issues that affect the entire system. For example, one woman's host complained that the child alters were hungry and crying. When questioned, she replied, "The bulimic one threw up after lunch again so the kids are all still hungry." We had to negotiate with the bulimic alter who did not realize that her actions affected others in the system.

Other DIDs have reported complaints about certain personalities because "this one is too religious," "that one is too angry," "another one is too wimpy," etc. Each alter's behavior can be observed by and affect other alters within the system whether or not there is co-consciousness. This causes the dissociative one to feel confused and "crazy" until they understand DID.

If you realize that a dissociative person could have no system, a simple system, or a complex system, you will better be able to minister to her. Without that recognition, you may underestimate the extent of her needs. If you understand that a system will generally have protectors, observers, memory and/or emotion bearers, and more, you will have a better idea of what to expect. If you run into programming and extensive systems, you will need additional training in working with ritual abuse survivors.

12

PRINCIPLES FOR WORKING WITH DISSOCIATIVE PEOPLE

1. You must be in a place of stability. The bulk of your personal issues must be well resolved. The added weight of ministering to a very needy person has the potential to wear you down and/or cause you to be impaired in your ability to respond effectively in ministry. Your unhealed issues will be the target that gets hit. If an angry alter reams you out, your unresolved anger and rejection issues will be triggered. If her issues are overwhelming and she becomes demanding, your unresolved fear or co-dependency issues will be triggered.

2. You must be able to lovingly establish boundaries in your relationship. Some of these tremendously traumatized people can be very needy and may attempt to encroach on your personal world. This is true especially if she has Borderline Personality Disorder traits. You must be able to establish parameters for timing and number of phone calls allowed, showing up in places you

frequent, etc.

Unfortunately, it often happens that the extremely dissociative person initially presents with normal issues and interacts within normal relationship limitations. The unsuspecting counselor subsequently discovers DID and will soon find the client demanding more time and attention. If the counselor is flexible and able to accommodate her, she will increase the demand. The counselor will have more difficulty enforcing her personal boundaries since they had already been breached by often clever manipulations.

Sometimes boundary keeping is difficult if there is no co-consciousness and one personality is unaware that another one had just called. One counselor finally told her client, "I'm sorry, but you have crises 24/7. You may only call me between 9 a.m. and 7 p.m. and only once a day. If it's too bad, call 911." It's not cold. It puts things into perspective for both parties.

Sometimes she will show up in public places such as stores or church. She may want to sit with you at church but child alters switch in and expect your attention. Be willing to say, "I'm so glad you come to the church I attend, but please sit somewhere that won't distract me from being able to worship."

3. Building trust is essential because of her extreme need to protect the core person as well as maintaining the secret of the dissociation. She may not have met very many people who have been trustworthy or knowledgeable. It may be wise to say something like, "I promise that I will never intentionally hurt you, but remember that I am human and might make a mistake or fail you in some way. Please forgive me ahead of time and help me understand your issues."

4. Educate, explain, give examples, give her resources describing dissociation, introduce her to other DIDs if mutually agreeable or if you have a group for that purpose. The more she knows about DID, the more she can work with you to help herself through the healing process.

5. If she doubts the dissociation, ask if you can try something that might seem silly: Ask if you can "look past" her (by looking into her eyes) and address the relevant protector, observer, or wounded part; and have that part let the host or you know what she hears. "Is there some part of Jane who knows about this memory?" Or "Is there a little Jane who kind of got stuck back there and still feels all the yucky feelings?"

6. Find an internal ally who will answer your questions and cooperate. (However, remember her

purpose and primary allegiance – the alter may deceive just a little.)

7. She will probably test you! All the time; every time; until she is healed and whole. Do not be insulted, just expect it. Walk in integrity.

8. It is sometimes necessary to find out if you are dealing with the core person. The personalities may lie or simply not know. Often you are working with a pseudo-core or strong protector or host with the same name as the original person. The presence of or absence of the original person is an indicator of the level of damage.

9. Some people work better with ministry directly between you and the dissociated parts; others prefer to have the core, host, or protector operate as the mediator between the two of you. Give her the choice and let her know some of the advantages and disadvantages of each approach.

Working directly with the alter is less tedious than going through a mediator who might omit some important data or may not be able to convey the depth of the emotions or other pain of the alter. One woman's host would say, "Okay, I'll step back now and let you talk to her."

Working with the host has other advantages. The host/core/protector stays apprised of whatever is going on with the various alters and can report some things that the alter may not mention. It also maintains her sense of control and feels safer to her. Be aware that sometimes the host may be somewhat controlling and may determine what is important and what should or should not be disclosed. You may miss a critical item because of this.

10. Explain the general long-term goals: Deliverance, healing of memories (body memories, emotional pain, mental anguish, forgiveness issues, release from deceptions, vows, curses, and judgments imbedded in the memory), and integration. These may happen simultaneously or as part of a healing progression.

Each of these goals are met only if traumatic situations are addressed and healed. Unfortunately, there is no blanket prayer that brings complete healing to many traumas and subsequent integration of all personalities that are involved in a more complex system. If there are one or two alters from one major trauma, however, it is possible.

11. Integration may be spontaneous and immediate or intentional and at a given time. It may also be gradual as alters become more acquainted with each other and their healing and deliverance is completed. God is very gracious to accommodate and customize each situation.

A woman who wore contact lenses reported very blurry vision after healing and integration of child alters and was unable to safely drive herself home after sessions. She asked God to integrate them while she was sleeping at night.

12. If possible, intentional integration should not be done until and unless an alter is healed of all body memories, emotional pain, and delivered of all strongholds and demons. Always have the agreement of the personalities involved and affirmation by the Lord prior to integration.

13. Appeal to the injustice of having to live with less than God's best and original intention for her life; especially in the face of fear and reluctance to change through healing and full integration. Recognize that living by dissociation is her "comfort zone." Facing life fully integrated can be intimidating when dissociation is all she has known.

One woman was astounded that it was normal to feel more than one emotion at a time. "I only felt anger. I don't know what to do with sadness or even happiness. That was someone else's job."

14. Believe. She may tell you some things that seem preposterous. It is her reality and has an impact on her life. Regardless of whether something happened to her exactly as she remembers or not, it will still impact her as if it did.

This is similar to anyone who encounters a snake on a trail and reacts. The body will pump out adrenaline to allow for the fight-or-flight response. If it was actually a crooked stick that just looked like a snake, there will be an identical physiological response whether it was a snake or a stick.

15. Body/muscle memory. *The body never lies.* When she describes a visceral response to a memory, or physical symptoms (pains, rashes, nausea, etc.) appear; know that something from her past caused it. The interpretation may or may not be accurate, but the body/muscle memory is always going to be accurate. She feels what she feels.

One woman described her "irrational" disgust of her uncle. "I have these images, but I'm not sure if I'm making it up. My skin crawls and I just want to run." When her muscle/body memory was affirmed and validated, a five-year-old part that held the incest memory emerged, and she was able to be healed, and integrated. Then the adult woman knew that she did not make it up and that her images were accurate and her emotional reaction to the uncle was reasonable.

16. Negotiate. Do not ever bully or coerce or manipulate any part into anything. Resistance on their part is your clue that there is another issue that must be resolved. That issue may need to wait until

other issues are dealt with first, or that part may need to feel safe prior to working with you.

Ask open ended questions such as, "What would happen if we looked at that memory?" "What would happen if what you suspect is true?" Address subsequent issues that arise from her answers to these kinds of questions.

17. Listen. Listen to what she is telling you. Listen to what she is *not* telling you. Ask the "why" questions to help her process objections, statements, misinterpretations, deceptions, vows, curses, judgments, emotions, and so on.

18. Help her establish an external support network. You cannot be her only support. She may have many objections, but she also needs trusted people from her family, community, church, place of work, neighborhood, or a group like Celebrate Recovery.

Those potential support people should be entrusted only with that which they can handle. If, for instance, a survivor tells a co-worker her entire history and that she has multiple personalities, she will likely be ostracized or ridiculed or perhaps lose her job.

19. Be prepared to be "fired" or accused of a negative motive. Some part(s) may only have partial understanding of things discussed. Other

parts will have an opposite response from the response that was expressed at a session.

One woman "fired" her counselor because the counselor "didn't discern that the child alter was lying." The counselor did question the issue, but that was not how the host remembered the dialogue. Partial co-consciousness might have been the cause. Demonic interference may have been a factor. Priorities of the counselor and the counselee may have been different.

Another woman noticed that there was an engagement ring on her counselor's finger. The counselor said nothing about it, but the woman expressed excitement for the counselor. There was then a very brief discussion. At the next session, the counselee said that it was difficult because she was single and the counselor was being insensitive by going "on and on" about her engagement. The counselor was baffled by the two different responses until she realized that there were different alters responsible for the differing points of view.

20. Pray. Open with prayer. Pray about specific issues. Pray for the healing of memories and the alters that carry them. Pray when there is confusion or uncertainty about what to do next. Pray for blessings in closing prayers. Pray without ceasing.

Some practitioners are prohibited from addressing spiritual issues in their sessions or their clients may be opposed to addressing spiritual matters. It is necessary to address mental, emotional, and behavioral issues, but spiritual issues must also be addressed to bring complete healing. As beings comprised of spirits, souls, and bodies, healing would be incomplete without addressing all aspects.

13

BREAKING DISSOCIATIVE STRONGHOLDS

These principles and approaches to specific issues have been effectively used to help dissociative people come to unity and internal cooperation; and eventually to healing and wholeness. The core person can use these principles with the other personalities. Personalities can use them to minister to other personalities and to the core person as well.

Lie of multiplicity

The lie of multiplicity embraces the deception that there are many separate people who all just happen to be living inside the same body. There was some cosmic mistake and they just have to live with it. Demons will help maintain this faulty perception and the lie of multiplicity.

One personality can believe that she can commit suicide, for example, and it will not affect the other parts or the core person. That part is completely dissociated emotionally and mentally. She believes that she can die and the rest of the personalities will continue to live. She may also be convinced that upon death, she can go to hell while the rest of the personalities will go to heaven or vice-versa.

A very effective negotiation with a resistant or skeptical part is simply to ask permission to ask Jesus to bring her the truth about the multiplicity. She may resist, but you can point out that if you are wrong, she has only lost a little time. Assure her that nothing, including the dissociation, will change until she chooses to make changes.

The dissociation is *not* a lie. The dissociation is both a neurological and a soul level event. At the time of the trauma, the person did separate from the pain. The core and all the dissociated parts are, and always have been the same person. God knit her together in her mother's womb. She is one body, one soul, and one spirit. God's promise is redemption, restoration, and recompense for all that Satan has corrupted.

Dispelling the lie of multiplicity will not necessarily mean that immediate integration will result from breaking this stronghold, although there may be some spontaneous integrations. It is necessary for the lie to be dispelled or else the alter will see no reason to integrate without the truth that she came from the original person.

The same brain and mind that belongs to the core person is the mastermind behind all the alters. *Alters have no attribute that they did not receive from the core person.* The alters may develop and mature, but it is done within limits of the attributes given by the original person.

Take authority

There may be some resentment on the part of alters who have borne pain for the original core person, however, there comes a time when the core person must take authority (NOT control) over the alters as the one who is ultimately responsible before God. This is especially critical if a personality threatens to do something harmful to self or others.

One woman grasped this principle and made an announcement to her entire system, "Listen up everybody! We're done going our separate ways. I just want to let you know that I really appreciate what each part has done on behalf of everyone else, especially me, but you don't have to carry the pain anymore. Let's take this mess to Jesus and let's get healed." Many of the parts responded positively. Many were relieved. They were tired of carrying their burdens.

Sometimes the internal parts need to be given direction. Sometimes they need to know that they are appreciated. Sometimes they need to know that someone is there to help them. Sometimes they need to know that they have another option available. They are generally very ready to cooperate when they are given reasonable options. If there is lack of cooperation, then that personality should be encouraged to voice objections and/or fears about the changes since that is an indication of an unresolved issue.

Take responsibility

The host, core, or other part must deal with any sin committed by the body no matter which alter did it. Confessing the sin and receiving God's cleansing as a responsible believer often breaks the offending alter's heart and brings reconciliation between the alter and the core and/or host.

One woman reported that when she prayed and confessed the sin of adultery that was committed decades earlier by a personality whose "job" it was to be promiscuous, that promiscuous personality was then grieved because the original core person took responsibility for the sin. It was a turning point for that personality to finally receive healing and integration. Often, personalities think that they are too bad to be forgiven.

Take ownership

This principle goes along with taking responsibility and is applicable to dissociated and non-dissociated people. God has given stewardship of spirit, soul, and body to each person. Everyone reacts in some way to abuse and/or trauma. Taking ownership of one's own response(s) is a big step toward healing.

Passivity and blame-shifting are counter-productive. To look back and blame the perpetrator for whatever consequences came from the abuse and/or trauma only encourages bitterness. It takes a level of healing and maturity to come to a point of being able to own one's own past responses and present situation and allow God to redeem it all.

It may be helpful to ask, "What would you be like if *that* never happened?" The surprising answers are often things like, "I wouldn't have the character that I do." "I wouldn't be as resourceful as I am now." "I wouldn't be able to minister to others like I can now. They wouldn't give me a chance unless they knew that I knew an inkling of their pain." "I wouldn't have the I.Q. that I have."

Writing exercises

Since the right side of the brain controls the left side of the body, and vice versa, a person can use this principle to tap into memories. Writing will stimulate the side of the brain opposite of the hand that is used for writing.

If there is no "visual" memory it can be very useful for the person to write open ended questions using their right hand – stimulating the left side of the brain (the cognitive side) – and then put the pen into her left hand and write out the answer. If the memory was "misfiled" on the right side of the brain, it may be reached.

The core or host may write, "Does anyone know what happened when we had visitation at dad's house when we were five?" "Is there a part of me that's stuck at age five and knows about that visit to dad's house?" "Why do we have that funny feeling whenever we think about going to dad's house?"

The penmanship will probably be sloppy if one is not naturally left-handed, but it should yield an answer. It may feel as if the answer was contrived, but trust it enough to follow up with more questions and prayers. It may also yield a strong emotion such as fear or anger that was not previously felt. Follow those up with prayers asking the Lord to take you to the root of *this* kind of emotion. You may then be taken to a memory or you may need to ask for more illumination from the Lord. Keep asking. Keep praying.

Specific prayers

Pray that the core and each alter will see their heart as God sees it. Opening the eyes of the "blind" brings hope and reconciliation since there are usually feelings of guilt, shame, regret, taintedness, and so on.

Pray for specific alters to "see" through the core or host person's eyes. This insight will bring some reconciliation and the "seeing" experience will allow alters (who nearly always have their outlook limited) to have increased understanding about their whole life.

The alters, host, and core will all benefit by praying for the specific memories, feelings, issues, etc. of each other.

Pray for unity and removal of specific barriers to unity. (Eph. 2:11-22.)

Pray that God would bring alters up-to-speed, especially if they have not been out for years.

There are sample prayers later pertaining to these and other issues. Dissociative strongholds exist and remain for many of the reasons addressed in this chapter. Addressing them through prayer after discussing the issues and gaining trust and permission is an effective way to attain healing. The continual prayer on your lips can be as succinct as, "What's next, Lord?" Trust Him to direct your thoughts and prayers.

Addressing intolerable conflicts

Intolerable conflicts represent some of the strongest glue that holds dissociation in place. Dissociation allows for two equal and opposite "truths" – My family cherishes me/my family neglected me. My father loves me/my father molested me.

One woman, after experiencing a flashback about an early incest event reacted with disbelief and had an internal argument. "No! My daddy would never do that." "Yes, he did." She agonized and searched for any other explanation. "I read it somewhere." "I heard it on the news." "Someone told me their story." "No, it happened."

She finally had to stop denying the truth, stop her denial, and face the excruciating anguish. "Anyone but daddy! Please, God, anyone but him!" With the help of her counselor, she was able to forgive him, work through the memory, and move on to a measure of reconciliation with her father.

14

INTEGRATION

As previously stated, integration is the opposite of dissociation. It is a huge step in the healing process but it is not the final step. Once someone is fully integrated, there will still be "normal" issues with which to deal.

One woman who was recently fully integrated called about a relatively minor issue. Her counselor congratulated her and assured her that this was normal. The woman was clearly outside of her old comfort zone of dissociation and was somewhat overwhelmed. When asked if she wanted to go back to doing life as a DID, she hastily declined and laughed. "I'll get used to it one of these days."

The following is a letter from a woman who expresses most of the concerns that dissociative people have about integration:

"There's something I'd like to ask you about concerning when everyone has merged and the 'real' [Jane] has

emerged from hiding. I want to know if she will "recognize" you and you'll mean as much to her as you do to me. Once the healing is complete, Lynda, will this affect 'our' friendship? Can we remain friends and continue a friendship? Will the real Jane know the same things the others do and I do? Will she have the same handwriting as me or a different one? Will her personality be so totally different that it will be noticeable to others? Will she know her kids… her family… her friends? Just how drastic of a change is it going to be? I worry about these things and it makes me a bit leery about merging. Just what you wanted to hear, right? Sorry! Maybe I shouldn't be so anxious, I know. It's all so new to me! The way things are now… THIS IS ALL I KNOW!!!! Thanks for your patience."

Variations on these questions and concerns expressed in the above letter have been asked by countless dissociative people. Transitioning from what they considered to be normal to a new normal of wholeness is a lot to absorb. When asked if they would like to go back to dissociation, one hundred per cent said with no hesitation, "No way!"

Many dissociative people are astounded when they realize that not everybody is dissociative and that Dissociative Identity Disorder is an anomaly. It is often true that dissociative people are drawn to each other without realizing their common bond. It is likely that many of their family members have high dissociative ability and have also experienced trauma, perhaps at the hands of the same perpetrator and are also dissociated.

It can be helpful to explain dissociation and integration with simple illustrations or analogies. Think of a stream that flows free, clear, and strong from its source. Then someone throws boulders or rocks into it and causes the stream to be divided, diverted, and dammed up in places. Boulders and rocks correspond to the various traumas. Integration occurs after the boulders are removed and the stream can flow strong and unimpeded as it was intended to do.

Perhaps someone can relate to a pail of clear water. Dirty rocks are thrown into it and droplets are splashed out of the pail. The droplets represent dissociated traumatic parts with their memories while cleansing the water and returning the droplets to the pail represents the healing journey.

Always bear in mind that dissociation became necessary because of overwhelming and/or unprocessed trauma. Dissociative blockades are erected because of the need for denial not only of the pain, but the fact of the dissociation itself.

When there is no longer a need to protect the painful places because they have been healed, integration can occur. When there is no longer a need to hide or deny the dissociation itself, integration can occur. When the denial side personalities can face their utter rejection or other intolerable conflicts especially by significant family members, integration can occur.

One healed and integrated survivor said it well: "Sometimes it all seems like a dream. Sometimes I want to go into denial because it is unbelievable; but what keeps me tuned into the present is the explanation that it gives to my past. My past and dissociative behavior cannot be overlooked, forgotten or swept under the rug. For me, remembering how I used to think, act and behave is what grounds me to the present."

Integration is a reversal of the dissociation. Again, other common synonyms for integration are fusion, association, blending, re-knitting, joining, melding, jelling together, going back into, or having each part take their rightful place in the person. These terms range from those generally accepted in the counseling community to those coined by dissociative people.

Be sure that there is clear understanding as to meaning of any terms you use. Use whatever terminology makes sense to the dissociated person with whom you are working. Effective communication is essential.

There is no set formula for integration. It will

reflect each individual person's preference. Twenty-five years ago, when I was working with my first dissociative person, we would have a personality integrate almost immediately upon discovering that part because we naively thought that integration was the mark of healing.

What we discovered was that the dissociated personality integrated complete with all the body memories, mental anguish, emotional pain, strongholds, and sometimes demonic oppressors. The host personality or other protector who integrated with the newly integrated part was then traumatized by the other part's issues.

She exclaimed, "It's like slam dancing!"

We learned that it was prudent to work with the traumatized dissociated personalities and process all the issues associated with body and soul, as well as spiritual matters prior to integration. While it could still be disturbing for integrated personalities to receive "new" bits of information, integration became much less disruptive and previously unknown history became much easier to accept.

Perception of her own integration by the dissociated person will also take place on a continuum from very subtle clues to very vivid indicators. These people are generally very visual, imaginative, and creative; and God uses those qualities in their integrations to convey truth in a way that is meaningful to them.

Remember, too, that this aspect of healing is no different than any other in that we *always defer to Jesus* when it comes to the manner, the timing, and who integrates into whom.

Be aware that integration may cause a temporary disruption for the core or host person. It may affect their vision (child alters didn't need glasses, but the adult does, so integration affects vision until it stabilizes) or their coordination (child level coordination and experience is different than adult) or other skills (driving, hand-writing, social interaction, etc.).

This can be distressing for the host personality, and yet, it can be reassuring because there is tangible evidence that something has occurred. It is prudent to let her know that there is no right or wrong way to integrate and that whatever she senses is accurate.

Many first-time integrations will be questioned. "I just saw something like a pie that was cut into a bunch of pieces and then suddenly the pie was whole." "I felt this movement in my belly, like everyone in there was moving over to make room." Quite often, she will state what she has seen or felt or sensed and then ask something like, "Did I make that up? Is that for real?"

Ask her if she senses the presence of the personality or group of personalities that were supposed to have been integrated. If she cannot sense them, then you can be assured that they have been successfully integrated. If there is no sense of the personalities having been integrated into the host, it may well be that they integrated into a protector or the original person and the host would not sense anything different.

If there remains doubt, then ask Jesus to affirm the integration. Rarely, a personality will say that she will integrate, but then during the prayer for integration, she changes her mind and disappears. The host personality is usually aware of this and can report it to you. In this case, you must assume that the part changed her mind because she still has other issues remaining.

Again, be aware that integration of alter to alter or alter to core or host will bring a mutual combining of memories, knowledge, and emotions. The Lord may integrate a part into the original core person. He may "consolidate" a group of alters into the protector of that group. He may integrate in a way that is not felt or sensed. Sometimes the only indication of integration is the absence of the part(s).

Even when the Lord takes the "sting" out of the

memories, there may be an impact on the core person as she regains another chunk of her life and begins to realize just how wounded she was or just how unloved and rejected. Because of this, it is important that each alter is fully healed prior to integration to minimize the impact on the system.

The following describe some of the common ways integrations can occur:

Spontaneous integration

Spontaneous integration usually follows healing of an individual personality or a group of alters. It may occur immediately or at some later time. Sometimes they integrate before the prayer for healing is even finished.

The host or core person may notice that someone is missing and sense that integration has occurred. Many times, there will be awareness of the integration and reports of feeling more whole, complete, richer, fuller, better, right, and so on.

She might report, "It feels like someone came in." Some have reported physical sensations inside their head or some area in their abdomen. One person said, "I could feel the others moving over and making room inside. They all kind of adjusted and then settled into place." Others have described seeing images of three-dimensional puzzle pieces fitting together.

In the situations in which Jesus has been healing alters in stages (see below), He will often bring a spontaneous integration when sufficient healing has taken place for them. Spontaneous integration can take place during a ministry session, during sleep, or at any other time.

Mass integration

These marvelous people have tremendous senses of humor. One witty woman cracked, "Mass integration is for the Catholics; I'm a Baptist, let's have an alter call."

Group integration is seen most often in those who have more extensive systems. It is the grace and mercy of God which "short-cuts" the process so that every memory, issue, feeling, etc. of each alter does not have to be addressed. It seems that the ones who are integrated en masse are some of the nameless, numberless ones that are vaguely referred to by the key alter or protector of that related group of alters. Obtain permission of the spokesperson of that particular group to pray on behalf of all who are in that group. Be sure of complete healing prior to integration.

Sometimes she will report, "They're all gone!" Or, "I think one is still out." She may or may not visualize the process. One woman reported, "Wow! It's like a whole herd of them came rushing through the gate!"

They are often astonished at the numbers of alters that they were not even aware of originally. Others are aware of numbers but do not want anyone else to know. It is not important to have a head count. Many DIDs feel embarrassed and overwhelmed by the numbers.

Help them maintain their dignity by not asking for unnecessary details.

Sometimes a personality holds out because of fear that threats against her would be carried out, therefore, she will not speak about her memories and thus, will be unable to process them and be healed. Many abusers threaten them (usually a child alter) with harm to her or to loved ones if she tells anyone. Pray for the alter to perceive her present circumstances – current age, distance from the abuser, capabilities, and so on.

Sometimes a personality does not want to give up her autonomy. Ask questions and address the issue that emerges. There is a reason for her hesitation, especially if she is a protector who does not fully trust in the Lord's protection.

Pray *big!* Especially when dealing with highly

fragmented systems, pray extensively. Pray that the healing will apply to all alters who have any direct connection with a particular alter or group with whom you are ministering. Pray that any other alter who has been listening in and agreeing would be included since they sometimes think they need permission. Pray that any other alter with these or similar pain, memories, etc. would also be included and that reciprocal healing will take place in them.

Intentional integrations

Intentional integrations are the result of situations in which an alter or group of alters have already received healing. There may be uncertainty about whether or not to integrate at this point or to remain dissociated for a while. There may be uncertainty about full integration into the original person or integration into a protector or section leader. Address each issue as it comes up.

The following could be made into a general flow chart for navigating intentional integration after an alter or group of alters has received healing by asking the alter or representative of the group the following questions:

1. Do you sense any remaining physical or emotional pain? Do you sense any demonic strongholds or demonic oppression?

If the answer is NO, ask the Holy Spirit to confirm this and then pursue integration.

If the answer is YES, ask Jesus to reveal the root of the pain or demonic stronghold and work through the issue(s) until everything is completely and satisfactorily addressed.

2. Do you have any sense as to whether or not you should integrate? Do you have peace about whether or not you should integrate?

If the answer is NO, defer to Jesus, He will let her know or give her peace.

If the answer is YES, I/we should integrate; ask Jesus to do it according to His timing and placement of personalities into the original person or into another appropriate personality.

3. Do you want to integrate?

If the answer is NO, ask Jesus to inform the alter(s) of their new role (usually protecting in a godly way rather through anger, for example) in the system until the alter is ready and willing to integrate at the most beneficial time. Jesus may want them to rest for a while before integration.

If the answer is YES, ask Jesus to integrate them according to His timing and placement.

Most often, it is the protectors who will remain in their role for a time. They will usually be among the last to integrate. The core, host, or key protector will often have that insight and may say something like one of the following statements. "When I go in, it will be all done." "She will be the last one." "I know I'll be whole when she goes in."

Integration by stages

In a sense, all integration is by stages. The first stage is just becoming aware of the existence of the alters and the system of personalities. This is followed by praying through issues, and finally, praying for integration.

It is important to remember that some personalities may have a gap between praying through their issues and final integration. It may be hours, days, or more in some cases. God often chooses to have a time period for some alters to become refreshed and healed prior to completing the integration.

God is infinitely creative and we are created in His image. He has given gifts of imagination and the ability to visualize things. Jesus used parables to illustrate His teachings. We know that a picture is worth a thousand words. These God-given word pictures are very real and often very vivid to those experiencing them. The Holy Spirit may use a Scriptural image. The following are some common examples that have been reported by more than one dissociative person:

Meadow

Very often, Jesus will use the imagery of Psalm 23:2, 3. *"He makes me lie down in green pastures; He leads me beside quiet waters. He restores my soul…"* There will be a peaceful meadow, quiet streams, rocks to sit on, and so on. Jesus will manifest His presence there. He often brings out deeply wounded child alters and heals them there prior to their integration.

Some have reported child alters sleeping in soft beds, lush grass, or in Jesus' arms. Some describe toys and other child alters to play with in the meadow. It seems that Jesus is giving them a childhood that is as carefree as it should have been as they were growing up. Many of these alters seem to have been terrified by enclosed places (basements, rooms, closets, etc.) and really love the absence of walls.

Building

"… for I go to prepare a place for you…" John 14:2. Sometimes, the imagery of a tent, cabin, building, room, or some other safe and private place is used.

They report that Jesus has built it for them and brought them there. These alters seem to need the security of a place of their own. These alters love the safety of the walls.

I've heard reports from some who had places for the "little kids" with teddy bears, dolls, etc. and another for the teens with "cool stuff." Others have a safe place where they can rest, recover, and be recompensed for their losses. Again, these images may have little meaning to us, or may even seem irreverent, but they are very meaningful to the child alters who experience these creative kinds of healings prior to their integrations.

River

Several have related the images of Psalm 36:7 – 9. *"How precious is Your lovingkindness, O God! And the children of men take refuge in the shadow of Your wings. They drink their fill of the abundance of Your house; and You give them to drink of the river of Your delights. For with You is the fountain of life; in Your light we see light."*

Some have had alters go to the river with Jesus, receive healing from body memories, emotional pain, and mental anguish in the river and just kind of float down the river and into the core person.

One very shame-filled person believed that she

was not clean enough to go directly into the river so her alters had to be cleansed in the fountain first and then they could go into the river. She reported that they played there until integration, usually during sleep at night.

Jesus

"And they were bringing children to Him so that He might touch them... And He took them in His arms and began blessing them, laying His hands on them." Mark 10:13, 16.

Some have described meaningful conversations with Jesus prior to being "absorbed" into Him and then they emerge clean and healed after being *in Christ* and being placed into the core person.

Others have described Jesus standing between the two dissociated parts and hugging them together to integrate them.

In another case, an entire group was "jelled" together by Jesus and then went into the core.

It is critical that guided imagery is NOT used. Do not say, "I want you to picture _____." Do not use leading questions or suggestions. Be aware of their people-pleasing tendencies as well. This must come from God.

Trial integrations

Sometimes there is reluctance by the core person and/or one of the alters to integrate. Usually the alter is the one who is hesitant. The most common objections are that they don't want to "die" or "disappear," they don't want to lose their autonomy or control, or they are afraid of the change. They may feel rejected or that what they have done for the core will be forgotten. Take the time to address these issues and look for vows or deceptions behind them which keep them from agreeing to integrate.

Remember that dissociation is all she knows. Transitioning to the normal end of the dissociation continuum can be frightening. All the questions that were posed in the letter at the beginning of the chapter are very real. Change is difficult. Leaving a comfort zone can be very intimidating even when it was not all that great.

If there is a sense that everything is dealt with that can be, and the Holy Spirit seems to affirm that, suggest a trial integration. Remind them that they split out once; they can do it again if they want to. Tell them that others have done a trial and once they integrated, they really didn't want to split out again because their fears were addressed. Warn them that it is different, but it is better for them as well as the core. Tell them that this is a very effective way to protect the core from the inside.

Suggest a trial integration of as little as one minute. She may be willing to try integration until the next ministry session. In the rare case of one who does the trial integration but decides to remain dissociated, ask the Lord to reassign this part's role in the system. If they remain separate, there is a good reason that may not become apparent until much later in the healing process. Quite often the trial integration does become a successful permanent integration.

Forced integrations

This is a very rare situation and done for the good of the whole. The following situations will serve to illustrate some circumstances that have warranted this action:

An eight-year old boy kept splitting off new alters between ministry sessions. He was told that he may not do that anymore and that all the ones he made that week had to go back in. He responded to the counselor's authority and integrated them immediately. He was also told that the more he made, the longer he would have to spend his Saturdays doing counseling. He finally decided to allow the Lord to heal the original trauma and then he made them all come in and integrated over fifty alters in just a matter of minutes.

A severely abused woman's host personality

reported that she was aware of another alter's plan to do something destructive. A half-joking suggestion was that the next time she saw that alter, she should tackle her and integrate. She did. Then she understood the fears and issues that drove that alter, worked them out, and split her back out again without the destructive drive.

In the case of preverbal alters, the host or some protector may report a little one in distress. First, try praying in agreement with the core or alter for the Lord to bring healing. Many times, He will bring healing first and then the little one can be integrated as usual. If the Lord chooses not to heal, it is for a purpose, usually for obtaining knowledge of the trauma.

Pray and ask who should integrate with the baby. The Lord will appoint someone or a protector may volunteer and they will integrate as we pray. Once integrated, that verbal part will know the issues of the infant and will then be able to pray specifically about those issues.

One woman's protector integrated with a preverbal infant. Once that was done, the protector understood that the distressed infant was hungry. "I want a cheeseburger!" the protector exclaimed immediately after the prayer for integration. She understood the reason that the pre-verbal personality was distressed.

Sometimes a very mature and assertive person will take responsibility for and authority over her parts. She will gently thank the parts and then inform them that their "job" is done and that they can let Jesus heal them and integrate them for the good of the whole.

The following comments from those who have experienced integration give additional insight into the changes that challenge those who are being healed and integrated:

"I can definitely feel myself taking up space, like I am a real person."

"I have to get used to my voice – it seems different."

"I heard Jesus say, 'I am knitting them together.'"

"I feel like I'm all lined up again."

"I don't know if it happened or not… I see nature scenes: clouds and water splashing, overlapping…" Later she confirmed that the alters were absent and she felt more complete.

Integration marks a big step in the healing process of a dissociative person. It means that healing of emotional pain, body memories, and traumatic memories has been accomplished. Strongholds have been demolished and demons renounced for individual personalities or groups. The original person will grow stronger with every healing as all the attributes, strengths, character qualities, etc. that she dissociated out will be integrated back in.

15

SAMPLE PRAYERS

The following sample prayers are intended to give you an idea of how to pray in certain situations that come up with DID counselees. They are written assuming a female named Jane is being prayed for. Customize them as needed.

Be sure that the appropriate healing has been accomplished prior to some of the prayers for integration. Some of the prayers you may pray for the person, other prayers they should pray. In either case, it is good to pray in agreement.

DISPELLING THE LIE OF MULTIPLICITY

Father, we ask You to bind the enemy so that it cannot interfere in any way, shape, or form. We plead the blood of Jesus the Christ over every aspect of Jane: spirit, soul, body; mind, emotion, and will. There are some parts of Jane who have been convinced that they are separate people who just happen to inhabit the same body.

Father, Your Word says that You have made Jane with one spirit, one soul, and one body. We ask You to bring Your truth about this matter, in whatever way You choose, to each part of Jane as well as the core person. Let this truth set them free from any deceptions or confusions about the lie of multiplicity and affirm the truth of the dissociation. We pray this in the name of Jesus Christ of Nazareth, amen.

GENERAL PRAYER FOR INTEGRATION

Father, we come before You with the knowledge that You have healing in Your wings. You have brought healing to the dissociated parts of Jane. She now desires to be made whole. You knit her together in her mother's womb and we are asking that You would do a re-knitting where there has been splitting.

We pray that any residual pain in any memory in any part of her mind would be healed before you bring this wholeness. We pray for Jane's separated parts as Paul prayed for the fragments of Your body, the Church. In Christ Jesus, you who were far off have been brought near by the blood of Jesus Christ. We declare that Jesus is Jane's peace and the One who makes all parts into one, and breaks down the barrier of the dividing wall by abolishing the enmity. In Christ the parts are made into one new, whole person, thus establishing peace.

Thank You, Jesus for reconciling them in one body to God by the cross. Thank You, Jesus for preaching peace to parts who were far away and to parts who were near, because through Jesus, all parts have access in one Spirit to the Father.

So then, Lord, they are no longer strangers and aliens, but fellow citizens, having been built upon the foundation with Christ as the cornerstone in whom the whole building is being fitted together and is growing into a holy temple in the Lord.

You are a God of order; we bless You for removing the enemy's disorder. We also pray that You would make the adjustments to her wholeness rich and satisfying. We praise You for Your promise to bring beauty for ashes and to turn mourning into dancing. Hallelujah! What a Savior! Amen.

(Ephesians 2:11-22 describes the integration of the Jews and Gentiles in one Church. The above prayer is an application of the principles found in that passage.)

The above prayer is also a more detailed and extensive prayer and is useful to give a solid basis for integration. Be aware that most of the time the prayer for integration can be reduced to a few sentences as in the one below. Combine and/or customize them as needed.

"Lord, we believe this part is ready to integrate, would You please put her back into her rightful place and bring them unity in a bond of peace. Bless her with recompense for everything that the enemy has stolen from her. Please complete and correct anything we may have missed. Thank You, amen.

PRAYER FOR MASS INTEGRATION

Father, we come before Your throne of grace in the name of Jesus Christ. We lift up this group of alters who have received healing from their traumas. We ask that You bless them for bearing the pain of those events on behalf of the whole. We ask that You recompense them for everything that the enemy has stolen from them.

We pray that You would now complete and correct anything that we have prayed incompletely or incorrectly. We defer to Your wisdom to knit them back inside in the right place and at the right time so that there will be unity in a bond of peace for all concerned. We pray this in the name of Jesus the Christ, amen.

PRAYER FOR TRIAL INTEGRATION

Father, this part of Jane is not comfortable with the prospect of integration. She has consented to a trial integration of one minute. We ask that You release her from fear. We ask that You place her back inside in her rightful place for this time period. We ask that You give her better understanding of integration and then allow her to split back out again after the trial. Thank You for Your grace, amen.

PRAYER FOR FORCED INTEGRATION

Father, we have become aware that one of Jane's personalities is threatening to do something harmful that will adversely affect the whole. She is not willing to talk about it so we are asking that if she cannot be restrained You would appoint and affirm which part of Jane should integrate with her. We ask that we can further help this part by understanding what has driven the harmful urges. In Jesus' name, amen.

Following integration, she will understand the anti-social urges. Further prayers on that part's behalf may include choosing to forgive, renouncing verbal assaults, demolishing strongholds, renouncing demons, and so on.

Or

Father, we have become aware of a pre-verbal part of Jane that is in anguish. We believe that it would be beneficial for an adult part of Jane to integrate with her so that the issues can be sorted out and brought to Your throne of grace. We ask that You would now facilitate this integration in Jesus' name, amen.

PRAYER TO DISMANTLE LIES AND DECEPTIONS

God of all Truth, I have believed _____. I have said or thought this most of my life. It feels very true yet my logic says that it contradicts the principles of Your Word. I ask that You tell me what You think of that thought and bring me Truth that will set me free once and for all. I pray this in the name of Jesus who is the Way, the Truth, and the Life, amen.

Or

Father, I have believed _____. I choose now to declare what Your Word says about this. If it is necessary to go to the root of it, would You send Your Holy Spirit to lead me to that root so it can be eradicated once and for all, amen.

PRAYER TO SEE THROUGH GOD'S EYES

Father, this part of Jane believes that she is tainted, unworthy, guilty, irredeemable, unforgiveable, and more. Your Word says that You forgive and cleanse from all unrighteousness.

Father, she also believes that You are mad at her because of what she has done in response to the traumas she has endured and that she cannot be forgiven. Would You grant her the courage to look at her heart as You see it? Would you grant her the grace of being able to see her own heart? We pray this in Jesus' name, amen.

PRAYER TO SEE THROUGH CORE OR HOST'S EYES

Father, this part of Jane has had limited exposure to the totality of Jane's life. We ask that she would be correctly oriented to the present time and place and circumstances. We ask that You take the blinders off and allow her to see through the core/host's eyes so that she can understand how to work within the system for the good of everyone concerned. In Jesus' name, amen.

PRAYER FOR FORGIVENESS

Father, I confess that I have held a grudge against
_____ for saying/doing _____. Thank
You that You have provided cleansing from all
unrighteousness as I confess my sin of
unforgiveness towards him/her.

I ask that You now demolish the strongholds and
deliver me from oppressing spirits that have
plagued me because of my sin of unforgiveness.
Release me from any root of bitterness that brings
defilement to myself and others.

I choose now, as an act of my will, to grant an
unconditional grace to _____ that he/she has
not asked for and does not seem to deserve. Your
Word says that vengeance belongs to You. I will
stop trying to do Your job because righteousness
and justice are the foundations of Your throne. I
pray these things in the name of Jesus the Christ,
amen.

PRAYER FOR HEALING FROM ABUSE AND TRAUMA

Lord God, we come to Your throne of grace to
obtain mercy and grace regarding the abuse and
trauma sustained by the part of Jane that is stuck in
that pain. You are the same yesterday, today, and
forever. We ask that, as she focuses on that event,

she would see You there in that memory with her spiritual eyes, hear You with her spiritual ears, or just sense Your presence there. Bring her truth that will set her free once and for all from this pain.

We ask that You release her from every stronghold and tormenting spirit associated with _____ [name specific trauma] that has oppressed her since that time. We ask that You send those wicked spirits to a place where they will never afflict anyone ever again. Heal and seal this broken place with Your Holy Spirit.

We ask that You also cover her from the top of her head to the soles of her feet with Your cleansing blood and healing balm. Bring peace and ease, soothing and comfort to every part of her body that was traumatized. Release her from the body memories associated with whatever she saw, heard, smelled, tasted, touched, or felt. We ask that You heal any and all body memories associated with this trauma.

We also pray that You would correct and bring to balance any brain chemicals, adrenaline, hormones or any other natural or injected substance. We pray that You would heal every cell, tissue, organ, or system that was affected by the abuse/trauma.

We also pray that You would take the sting out of the memory and soothe her emotional pain. Release her from a spirit of fear and bless her with boldness and strength in You. We pray for Your goodness to be poured out on her so that she will be recompensed for her losses. Redeem her life from destruction.

Thank You for making all things new. Thank You for bringing beauty for ashes. Thank You that no weapon formed against her will prosper. We pray these things in the wonderful name of our Lord Jesus, amen.

(You may then want to follow up with a prayer for integration if all pain and discomfort is resolved for affected parts.)

PRAYER FOR HEALING OF SEXUAL ABUSE

Holy God and Father, we bring before You the sexual abuse _____ [molestation, incest, rape] that Jane sustained earlier in her life. She feels tainted by this sin. We ask that You cover that event with the cleansing blood of Jesus Christ.

We ask that You would cut in two the cords of the wicked and release her from every direct and indirect unholy union, soul tie, and flesh link associated with that event.

We plead the blood of Jesus over every stronghold created by that event and renounce and rebuke every foul spirit that has been given the so-called "right" to afflict. We ask You to send them with their entire hierarchies to a place where they will never oppress anyone again.

Please heal and seal this broken place by Your Holy Spirit. We also ask for healing of body memories and of any damaged tissue as well. Thank You that You restore purity and innocence as You remove humiliation, taintedness, and shame. We pray in Jesus' name, amen.

PRAYER REGARDING SEXUAL SIN

Holy Father, I confess that I have sinned by _____ [fornication, pornography, adultery, etc.] I know that Your Word says that if I confess my sin, You are faithful and just to forgive and cleanse me from all unrighteousness.

Father, I ask that You also cover me with the cleansing blood of Jesus and release me from the oppressing spirits and strongholds associated with the direct and indirect unholy unions, soul ties, and flesh links represented in those events.

I pray for restoration of purity and holiness in my thoughts, words, and actions. I pray in the name of Jesus, amen.

PRAYER FOR DELIVERANCE

Holy Father, I come to Your throne of grace in the name of Jesus the Christ. I ask that Your Holy Spirit would occupy any place in or around me which has been occupied by any spirit which is now causing these symptoms _____ [pressure, pain, queasiness, headache, etc.].

You have given us authority to cast out demons in the name of Jesus. I plead Your blood over this area of my life. If it is necessary to address the so-called legal right of this demon, I ask that You quicken that thought to my mind so I can renounce it. I pray these things in the name of Jesus the Christ, amen.

CONCLUDING REMARKS

Working with dissociative people can be very daunting for even the most experienced counselors and pastors. It is my hope that this work will have given you a basic understanding of this complicated coping skill that far too many have been forced to use early in life.

Dissociative people generally have several other life-dominating issues to further complicate their healing journey. Among them may be eating disorders, cutting, addictions, and anger issues. There are other resources written by Dr. Irons available on Amazon listed below.

Feel free to use the following contact information for sending questions or comments on the book to Dr. Irons at the following email: **ironsquillreader@gmail.com**

Counseling related E-Books by this author:

I am a Cutter, Please Help Me
Yo Soy un Cortador Ayudana Por Favor
Emotional Abuse and Verbal Assaults through
    Lies, Vows, Curses, and Judgments
Battling Anorexia, Bulimia, Binge Eating, Health
    Food Obsession
Panic and Anxiety Attacks
Heaven or Hell – Have I Lost My Salvation?
Mad at God, Self, and Others
Dissociative Identity Disorder
What's in Your Family Tree? Battling
    Generational Curses and Familial Spirits
Spiritual Gifts – Discovering Your Spiritual Gifts
Seeing, Hearing, Sensing God through His
    Brokenhearted Children

Fiction series of E-Books one through four by this
author:

Ritual Abuse – Autumn
Ritual Abuse – Winter
Ritual Abuse – Spring
Ritual Abuse – Summer

Made in the USA
Columbia, SC
27 September 2020